The Myth of
Natural Rights

PRAISE FOR *THE MYTH OF NATURAL RIGHTS*

Rollins has made hash of the logical connections in Rothbard's argument.

> — Robert Anton Wilson, *Natural Law*

An important book that every reader interested in libertarian theory should acquire.

> — Jeff Riggenbach, *New Libertarian*

Rollins does a fabulous job of making fools out of many a libertarian's philosophical heroes.

> — Justin Weinberg, *Guillotine*

An argument could be made that a book like this is potentially pretty damn dangerous.

> — Pat Hartman, *Salon: A Journal of Aesthetics*

Rollins' brief work is packed with enough analytical insight to send proponents of natural-law theory into hiding.

> — Jorge Amador, *The Pragmatist*

THE PORTABLE L.A. ROLLINS

The Myth of Natural Rights

Introduction by
TGGP

NINE-BANDED BOOKS +
UNDERWORLD AMUSEMENTS

ISBN-13: 978-1-943687-18-3

Thanks to:
Jeff Riggenbach & George H. Smith
for permissions to use their commentaries.

Mises Institute for use of
"On the Duty of Natural Outlaws to Shut Up."
Mises.org

Robert Anton Wilson Trust for use of "Natural Law, or Don't
Wear A Rubber On Your Willy."
RAWTrust.com

Sidney E. Parker Archives for use of "Letter."
SidParker.com

It is understood that SEK3 entered all of his work directly into
the public domain and eschewed belief in copyright. No represen-
tatives for the estate of Robert LeFevre could be found in the
production of this book, so we have erred on the side of
promoting his work rather than stifling it.

Nine-Banded Books
Charleston, WV
www.NineBandedBooks.com

Underworld Amusements
Baltimore, MD
www.UnderworldAmusements.com

Contents

Publisher's Preface

Kevin I. Slaughter (2019)

I'M VERY PROUD to be co-publishing this and other L.A. Rollins books with Chip Smith in a series we've dubbed "The Portable L.A.Rollins."

A decade ago, I wrote Chip an e-mail introducing myself, sending him links to my work, and letting him know that I'd love to work with him. He was warm to the idea. Chip was a freelance writer and blogger who, like me, had recently started his own publishing venture. Our interests overlapped in interesting ways. We agreed to trade books, which is always a good start.

A couple of weeks later, the books arrived at my doorstep. I didn't dig in right away, but I was in for a surprise when, on July 4th, 2009, I cracked the spine of the Nine-Banded Books edition of *The Myth of Natural Rights and Other Essays*. I was in the toilet, and I yelled out to my wife on the other side of the house, "What the shit?! Chip Smith thanks me in the introduction of this Rollins book?!"

So, for no reason you may care, that's where it started. The 2008 Nine-Banded Books reissue of *The Myth of Natural Rights* signaled the beginning of my publishing work with Chip. Since that time, I have worked with Chip on most of his books, and he has worked with me on some of mine. To now co-publish a revised and expanded edition of Rollins' contrarian classic as part of a series is a milestone in my own career as a small publisher.

The occasion is elevated by the fact that we were able to integrate the responses of George H. Smith, Jeff Riggenbach, S.E. Parker, Robert Anton Wilson, and several others into this new edition. *The Myth* remains an important book in my life, but Rollins' text was part of a larger conversation. To now revisit the voices of others who were part of this conversation—and who have influenced me at different stages of my life—is really quite satisfying. That most of them are arguing with each other makes it even better. The older I get, the more I realize that my worldview is contradictory, and maybe even capricious, regardless of how much pride I take in my "reason." It is, thus, somehow reassuring to observe these men who influenced me voicing disagreement on such fundamental issues. If nothing else, it reflects my own philosophical tensions.

¤

In his introduction to our new edition of *Lucifer's*

Lexicon, Chip wrote, "If you're of a certain age and of a certain intellectual temper, there's a good chance you'll recall your first brush with L.A. Rollins." When I read that, I smirked and nodded.

As a teenager, like so many others, I was always fond of anything with a Satanic motif. I still recall stumbling across, and then treasuring, Ambrose Bierce's *Devil's Dictionary* and how that experience primed me to snatch up the *Lexicon* as soon as I learned of its existence. I grew up in relative isolation, with little awareness of political movements, mainstream or dissident, so, while I enjoyed much of Rollins' book, it would take decades for me to begin unpacking many of his already obscure and dated references. I followed a very non-political path, eschewing anything that smacked of parties or movements or campaigns. I stuck to anthropology, psychology, and the category lovingly known as "misanthropology." While I became an autodidact, I was no genius, just intellectually enthusiastic and belligerent. I'd taken the term "Satanist" to identify my worldview. LaVey's philosophy was non-dogmatic enough and mixed a sense of dissidence with style. It was sexy and dangerous, at least in the abstract. In reality, I was a nerd that was constantly being told how well I'd do "if I just applied myself".

Eventually, in the '90s, I started bleeding into libertarian ideas, Ayn Rand and the like. I'd read George Smith's *Atheism: The Case Against God,* and it was "important" to my development. I was reading these writers outside of their "political" contexts, so sliding into that work was easy.

I'll admit, though, that even though I'd seen *Myth*, I hadn't read it until meditating in the ritual chamber with Smith's 2008 edition.

¤

In this new edition of *The Myth*, we have stripped away all materials not relating to the titular work and have included all the material relating to the eruption that the release of the book triggered among the "natural rights" libertarian crowd, specifically as it played out in the pages of Samuel Edward Konkin III's journal, *New Libertarian* (1978–1990).

This seems to be an evergreen debate among individualists of a certain disposition, and it strikes me as a renewal of a similar fracas that occurred in another journal, in another time.

Over the past few years, I have pursued a self-guided study of the history of individualist thought, particularly of the strain, first fully articulated by Max Stirner, known as egoism. In the United States of the early 20th century, one of the greatest advocates of Stirner was the anarchist publisher Benjamin R. Tucker, and it is in his journal *Liberty* (1881-1908) that we find evidence of a similar cleft that had developed between the advocates of natural rights, influenced by Herbert Spencer, and those amoralists who believed that "natural rights" were a ruse. According to the contrarians of the time, natural rights amounted to another mechanism of social control, no more beneficial than religious or political machinations, that merely acted as restraints on the sovereignty of the individual over himself.

Where *Liberty* had Lysander Spooner, Gertrude Kelly, and the poet J. Wm. Lloyd stumping for objective morality, roughly a century later it would be George H. Smith, and Murray Rothbard. Where *Liberty* had Tak Kak (James L. Walker), John Beverley Robinson, and Tucker himself as explicit advocates of egoism (and therefore contra natural rights), we could fast forward through the decades to find L.A. Rollins, Robert Anton Wilson, and Jeff Riggenbach staking essentially the same ground.

When the dust settled in *Liberty*, a schism was palpable. Many writers broke ties with the publication and with its egoist writers. I'm not sure if as much animosity was engendered by the *New Libertarian* forum, but the scrapping in the pages was lively and produced a more vigorous debate.

¤

So it is made explicit, I will note that Chip Smith's "Publisher's Preface" and TGGP's "Introduction" that immediately follow this preface are from the 2008 edition, *The Myth of Natural Rights and Other Essays*, which was published when L.A. Rollins was still alive. Since these introductory texts were written for an edition that contained *Lexicon* entries and some additional essays in addition to *The Myth*, some of the authors' references will not be directly relevant to the content of the present volume. They are nevertheless included in their entirety in order to flesh out the publishing history of *The Myth of Natural Rights*.

With that caveat, I will also point out that such

other writings by L.A. Rollins that are not featured in this book will return to print in separate volumes of "The Portable L.A.Rollins" series, along with a great deal of additional material.

¤

Louis Andrew Rollins was, and remains, an intellectual dissident *par excellence* in the sense that when he was in his prime, he was already a fringe figure that people felt the need to distance themselves from. Now, many of his ideas or interests have become completely taboo. He died in 2015. Chip Smith's "Introduction" in *Lucifer's Lexicon*, the first book in this series, will continue to be an important text for readers who want to know more about his life and work.

Kevin I. Slaughter
May 2019

Publisher's Preface
Chip Smith (2008)

IT WAS THE SUMMER OF 1988, and I had just flunked out of high school. With few prospects and no clue as to what I would do with "my future," I signed on for back-to-back summer classes. The idea was to belatedly collect my diploma, then buy some time by enrolling at a low-rung state college. I don't remember much about summer school, except that it was grim. I kept a low profile. I took the work seriously enough to secure the requisite marks. There was a lot of down time. So I read.

Two books are nestled up with my recollection of this time. The first was a dog-eared paperback edition of Ayn Rand's *Atlas Shrugged*. I remember it was set in miniscule typeface on age-oxidized high-acid paper. I would read a few pages and my eyes would itch from the strain. But having recently made my first acquaintance with the wily world of libertarianism, I was determined. I was seeking out the usual rites with the usual sense of pixilated teenage loner-nerd self-importance. Galt's Gulch was an unavoidable stop on that well-trod path.

So, I dutifully plowed through Rand's beloved magnum opus. And found myself hating it. The characters were humorless cartoons. The plot was straight-up silly. Even the ideas—the ostensible attraction—were presented with such inelegant, overwrought, didactic insistence as to induce a fugue. Somehow, I couldn't get past that heavyhanded prose, either. I still recall Rand's cloying, tic-like overuse of the term "inexplicable." Irritating.

When the eyestrain got the better of me, or when I had grown tired of being lectured—with all those "inexplicables"—about the self-evident virtues of Rachmaninoff and chain-smoking and objectivist epistemology, I would turn to the second book in my summerschool satchel, a bright-red Loompanics curio that I had borrowed from a friend. That book was *Lucifer's Lexicon* by L.A. Rollins. Ayn Rand would have hated it.

Styled after Ambrose Bierce's *The Devil's Dictionary*, Rollins' book was a strange bird. Where Bierce's acidic wordplay sought to expose the folly of humanity, Rollins' aphoristic spleen just as often pricked at the reality-challenged pretenses of libertarianism in its various flavors and guises. Real inside stuff. The "libertarian movement" was defined as "a herd of individualists stampeding toward freedom."

A "Randian" was a "Galt-ridden individual." "Egoism—the only 'ism' for me." I might have chuckled at that last one.

But there was something else about the book. Interlaced with the inside puns and one-liners, there were these digressive currents centering on the vicissitudes of Holocaust revisionism (that's the term they used back then). At the time, I didn't know a damn thing about *that* intellectual powder-keg. All I knew was that a TV miniseries had scared the shit out of me when I was a kid. Yet there it was. It seemed at times as though Rollins was in the revisionist camp himself. At other times, he seemed to hold revisionists out for wicked ridicule. I don't know if it occurred to me that this might not signal a contradiction. I just couldn't get a fix on it. I knew it was a huge subject. I knew what I was supposed to think. I let it go.

Anyways. After I said good riddance to Rand and shelved the *Lexicon*, I sent off my 7-Eleven money order and soon received a copy of Rollins' earlier book, *The Myth of Natural Rights*. There, I discovered a somewhat different voice—that of a working-class scholar. An accidental iconoclast. Rollins' bristling wit was on display but restrained in the service of a more focused argument. I read *The Myth* right on the heels of Rand and Rothbard, and I never really looked back. At least not through the same lens. In the wake of Rollins' shrewd work, those Aristotelian circularities tasted like stale beer. And Uncle Rothbard's pronouncements from on high reeked of nature-faking flummery. It was one of those books. Deceptively simple. You couldn't unthink it.

I still voted for Andre Marrou. Chalk it up to habit. If I were serious, I suppose I could have become a lobbyist.

Years went by, and I never heard much more about L.A. Rollins. Occasionally, I would see his satirical definitions tucked in the pages of obscure zines, soon to be forgotten. I spotted his byline in Pat Hartman's now-defunct journal *Salon* (not to be confused with the ad-laden webzine), where he was again trading zetetic riffs on the Holocaust bugaboo. Interesting. But no more books. I may have wondered what happened.

Around the time I was struggling to get Nine-Banded Books off the ground, I found myself re-reading *The Myth of Natural Rights*. By this time, I no longer gave much thought to libertarian metaphysics, but I found that the book held up well. After more than two decades, it still seemed marginally important. I went online to see if Rollins hosted a website. He didn't. After a few minutes of searching, I found an archived discussion thread where some old-school libertarians asserted that Rollins had gone off the deep-end—that he had become some kind of self-styled crypto-Nazi. Or something. I wondered if it might be true.

It wasn't, though I can't say that I cared. Loompanics had folded, and I didn't like the idea that L.A. Rollins' work would be left for dust. I wanted to republish *The Myth*, or at least to try. I had no idea how to contact the man, but I was in close touch with Bradley Smith, author of the first Nine-Banded Book, *The Man Who Saw His Own Liver*. Bradley knew Rollins from way back. He said he'd see what he could do. And so, after running the idea past Lou—that's the "L" in L.A.—Bradley put us in touch. Soon, a deal was in the offing. This is how it's done, I suppose.

The original idea was to simply re-publish *The Myth of Natural Rights*, perhaps with a new introduction and afterword. But when I spoke with Lou, he mentioned that he had been knocking off scads of new definitions for an updated edition of *Lucifer's Lexicon*. Maybe some of those could go in? I asked him about the Holocaust stuff, and he mentioned that he had written a (never published) piece for Sam Konkin's long-defunct *New Libertarian* magazine— something critical of revisionism. Maybe that could go in as well?

So Lou began sending me the material. Loads of it. In overstuffed double-stamped white envelopes, almost all of it in longhand (he isn't online). It was more than padding. There was enough new *Lexicon* material to justify a sequel. There was a deliciously bellicose bit of *fatwa*-bait called "An Open Letter to Allah." There were satirical verses and old essays from dodgy newsletters. Not all of it would make it in, but before long it was clear that the project had morphed into a collection. *The Myth* would retain top billing, but you want to give the kids their money's worth. As L.A. Rollins is fond of saying, *make the most of it*.

Of course, there was help along the way. There were folks who provided new content or who came through when I was scouring to verify obscure sources. Folks who offered encouragement and editorial assistance. Blurbs and permissions and free press. I want to thank them.

First and foremost, I want to thank Bradley Smith for setting things in motion. I want to thank TGGP for contributing a sharp and insightful new introduction to *The Myth of Natural Rights*. I want to thank Joseph Clagg for designing the cover. I want to thank Mike Hoy for allowing us to reprint the original Loompanics promotional copy for *The Myth*. I want to thank my wife, Erin, for assisting with the transcription. And, of course, I want to thank L.A. Rollins for everything.

I also want to acknowledge a number of other hominids who helped, whether they know it or not. My special thanks go to Michael A. Hoffman II, Pat Hartman, Victor Koman, Richard Widmann, Jonathan Price, Adam Parfrey, Charliqua X. Shabazz Elijah Jefferson Krafft, Aschwin de Wolf, Julie Herrada, Alex Kasavin, Jim Crawford, Kevin I. Slaughter, Andy Nowicki, Paul Bingham, Jack Malebranche, Peter Sotos, and David E. Williams.

CHIP SMITH
August 2008

Introduction: Against the Law

TGGP (2008)

IT DEPENDS ON WHAT YOU WANT. If you want to understand what Jefferson was thinking, read Locke. If you want to know how the modern libertarian movement got started, go ahead and wade through your Rand and Rothbard, or pick and choose from the wrecking yard of less benighted luminaries. It's a safe ritual and not without rewards.

On the other hand, if at some point you should wish to cut through all that carefully guarded architecture to see how the fragile edifice of libertarian ethics holds up under critical scrutiny, you can do no better than L.A. Rollins' short and shrewdly reasoned monograph, *The Myth of Natural Rights*. First published in 1983 by the late, great Loompanics Unlimited, it remains an essential touchstone for those who take their shibboleths with a shaker of salt.

A cursory review of the literature relating to "natural law" or "natural rights" is certain to reveal countless references to nonsense-peddler Jeremy Bentham's sharply tuned phrase "nonsense on stilts," but the most dedicated student must scour the footnotes to find a single citation of this deceptively slim explosion of the central tenet of modern libertarian theory.

No, you won't encounter the name "L.A. Rollins" in any philosophy course. He holds no academic position and has no acolytes to push his ideas into the ivory tower. Though he edited the marginally influential individualist journal *Invictus* for the better part of a decade and has written for the flagship libertarian magazine, *Reason*, Rollins remains *persona non grata* in the demimonde of cerebrally nuanced libertarianism.

This is a shame. Because for all its two-fisted truculence and bluster, *The Myth of Natural Rights* is perhaps the most important work on the subject to date. In a few concise and precise turns, Rollins soundly reduces hallowed libertarian axioms to phlogistons. Reading *The Myth* is like discovering that rare gadget that lives up to the infomercial hype. It renders every precedent text obsolete.

Without giving the game away, it is perhaps better to start out by saying what natural rights are *not* than what they are. If one were to begin a sentence with the phrase "natural rights are," that sentence would already be false. Natural rights are *not*. That they do not exist is the blunt thesis of *The Myth*.

Natural rights are the tooth fairies of political philosophy, claiming no more substance than the epiphenomenal gremlins inhabiting Daniel Dennett's car engine. Despite the carefully parsed semantic rigging, a "natural right" is nowhere to be found in nature, and unlike an actual legal or customary right, it confers no protection upon its claimant.

In their smug overconfidence, many exponents of this curious doctrine cast themselves as disinterested researchers who have "discovered" a pluperfect system of "natural laws" in some rarefied "science of liberty." The difference, of course, is that rocket science, done properly, results in actual rockets.

Steering past vast thickets of rhetorical buncombe, it soon becomes apparent that the metaphysical claims extolled by natural lawyers merit as much admiration as one might reserve for Wernher von Braun had he simply set aside his slide-rule and said, "Hey, wouldn't it be great if we could go to the Moon?"

Properly understood, natural rights are metaphors aping existent things. Or, stated differently, their existence—if the term may be allowed—is merely and necessarily metaphorical. This is the most salient point in *The Myth*, and Rollins hammers it to great effect. These dogma-drunk scholars who claim to have "discovered" something about the world in which we live are shown not to inform but to delude. They do not know; they merely wish.

A false statement, like "$0 = 1$," when permitted in mathematics allows one to prove anything one wishes. Similarly, permitting these purveyors of falsehood to claim their arbitrary and imaginary rights as metaphysically deducible axioms leads to myriad bogus results trajecting in every contradictory direction one cares or dares to imagine. Under the yoke of natural rights, various parties may trumpet their sundry demands on others whilst having neither the means nor the authority to enforce their compliance. Rollins shows this structure of "rights" to be without any real foundation. And that which lacks foundation must inevitably collapse.

Natural-rights theory finds its origin in the ideas of medieval scholastics, who thought that through reason, they could elucidate God's will over His subjects. During the Enlightenment, the idea of divinely endowed rights would assume new currency with Protestant thinkers, among whom we may count the Deists, who sought transcendent justification for their cherished liberal ideals. Thus, we come to see how malleable is this metaphysician's elixir, which can be custom-fitted to suit the vested interests of a modern liberal social order just as well as those of the illiberal Middle Ages.

In view of G.E. Moore's explication of the naturalistic fallacy, one might have expected ethical philosophers to stop churning out such circular appeals. But then, one would be operating under the assumption that ethical philosophers were vested with an interest in actual progress, in which case they could get jobs doing something more productive than boring students and playing incestuous word games with other philosophers. In the context of abstract philosophical disputation, logical flaws, and vague, meaningless babble can slide with little or no immediate consequence. Errors and mistakes do not blow up in one's face as engineering flaws do.

It distills to basic economics: when there is no cost to laziness and incompetence, you get a lot of it. And so, emboldened by their safely fortressed arrogance, natural-law gurus are thus free to coast on their reputations and take easy comfort in verbally bloated soap bubbles without overmuch concern. And if some reclusive morality-mocking pariah calls them on their shuck and jive, who's going to notice?

Though the torch of natural-rights rhetoric would eventually be passed on to fire-breathing atheist libertarians, at its core the doctrine has remained essentially religious in character. As such, it is deftly exposed by Rollins, who, like his amoralist-egoist forebear, Max Stirner, reveals the atheist "freethinkers" of his day to be God-intoxicated men in masquerade. The difference between Stirner's *The Ego and His Own* and Rollins' *Myth* is that the former is more deeply animated by the author's iconoclastic *elan* than by the rigorous strictures of analytical discourse. Where Stirner was mirthfully content to spin logomachian webs and toss Young Hegelianisms at Young Hegelians, Rollins sets out not to declare his defiance toward an impotent God but to carefully deprive believers of their deity. And Rollins' act of Deicide is accomplished in cutting measures, without pomp or apologies or safe, humanistic palliatives.

Theists and atheists alike may recoil from the

"amoralist" stance that Rollins adopts in the absence of rational appeal to transcendent moral verities, and Rollins' unrepentant flirtation with full-on nihilism won't be the only morsel to stick in the craw of some readers. For others, the line will be drawn around Rollins' altogether unnecessary, show-stopping declaration that he is a skeptic of "the Holocaust in general and the six million Jews supposedly killed by the Nazis in particular." Though he briefly implicates Hitler for his tacit appeal to something like a natural right to enslave conquered peoples, Rollins' casual dalliance with the most unseemly currents of contemporary crimethink will be enough to jar the sensibilities of many readers—readers who are constitutionally incapable of seeing beyond the neo-Nazi cartoon afterimages. Similarly, Rollins' attack on Rothbard's argument against race-based slavery could be read to imply covert support for the peculiar institution.

If such pronouncements linger in your mind strongly enough to poison the well, so be it. Run for the hills if you must. Because it is to Rollins' ultimate credit that he does not sugarcoat his message or attempt to associate his intellectual reputation with anything most libertarians would look upon with favor. Had he set out to present himself as a likable and agreeable sort of person, he might have sought the auspices of ISI, or Cato, or some other influence-peddling think tank. But Rollins refuses to don the good-guy badge. His iconoclasm is universal acid. Nothing is sacred.

It may strike some as ironic that Rollins reserves

his most strident attacks for those who, like him, call themselves "egoists," while proponents of more altruistic ethics—exemplified by Robert LeFevre—are cited with approval. But there are reasons. Randian "egoists," having decided it is in their interest to bind others with moral proscriptions, hastily set about flim-flamming their votaries into thinking they have no choice if they are to act rationally in pursuit of their own ends. This tactic stands in contradistinction to LeFevre's stance, which, out of selfless commitment to a moral code justified by nothing other than its own goodness, remains philosophically exposed to the unbound predations of the amoralist.

If Randian "egoists" recognize that their preferred ethical system rests on simple self-interest, Rollins turns this justification upside-down by showing how their vaunted "right to life" must lead to man's self-sacrifice and death. (By beating the Randians at their own game, Rollins betters Sidney Parker's deft unpacking of Ragnar Redbeard's *Might is Right*, whose bombastic power philosophy Parker reduces to comic spirals of self-contradictory moralizing.) For the altruist, the choice between egoism and preferential morality has already been decided in favor of the latter, and so it is to the "ethical egoist" that this combination must be shown to be incompatible. Rand and her followers are thus revealed as "bleeding-heart libertarians," no better than the liberals they mock.

It is likely that most readers of *The Myth* are going to be libertarians. Upon finishing, such readers will have a number of options before them. They may insist that Rollins is simply wrong and that the doctrine of natural law remains somehow unscathed. Considering the persistence of creationism, this would not be an unprecedented response to good evidence and argument. Alternately, they may claim that Rollins' critique does not take proper account of moral justifications marshaled under the mantle of utilitarianism or argumentation ethics, though this would probably be uncommon since it would mean shedding the last tethers of moral absolutism. They could abandon their commitment to libertarianism—and perhaps ideology altogether—adopting something akin to Jeffrey Friedman's more skeptical "post-libertarianism." Or they could push for an amoral contractarianism such as that suggested by Benjamin Tucker or David Gauthier. Surely, there are yet other options. Binge drinking, perhaps?

Whatever they do, one thing is certain: it will violate nobody's natural rights.

TGGP
March 2008

The Myth of
Natural Rights

Since late Neolithic times, men in their political capacity have lived almost exclusively by myths.
—James J. Martin

1

ONE OF THE MAJOR POLITICAL MYTHS of the modern age has been the myth of "natural rights," the myth of rights with which human beings are supposedly endowed by nature. This myth was enshrined in the American Declaration of Independence as well as the French Declaration of the Rights of Man. And although the myth has lost much of its power during the last two centuries, it nevertheless survives and in some regions even flourishes—in the fevered imaginations of contemporary libertarians, for instance.

"Natural rights"—variously referred to as "man's rights," "the rights of man," "human rights," "individual rights," "Lockean rights," or "moral rights"—are rights that people are supposed to possess simply because they are human beings. Or, to put it another way, natural rights are rights that people supposedly possess simply by virtue of their human nature. Since natural rights are supposedly possessed simply because one is human, such rights are therefore considered to be universal: possessed by all people. Furthermore, they are considered to be inalienable: not subject to being taken away. And, it is held, all people have the same, or equal, natural rights.

The myth of natural rights is an offspring of the related myth of natural law. As Murray Rothbard, "Mr. Libertarian," puts it, "'Natural rights' is the cornerstone of a political philosophy which, in turn, is embedded in a greater structure of natural law."[1] Similarly, Ronald Cooney sees the notion of natural rights originating in "the Roman Stoic idea of a 'law above the law,' of an unwritten law which precedes and is superior to man-made law."[2] This "superior" form of law is, of course, the "natural law." (This "natural law," it must be emphasized, is a moral law which prescribes how people *ought* to act. It is distinct from scientifically established laws, sometimes called "natural laws," which describe how natural phenomena regularly *do* act.)

Now what do I mean by calling natural rights "mythical"? Well, just as iconoclastic psychiatrist Thomas Szasz has said that mental illness is mythical and is really a fake or metaphorical illness,[3] so I say that natural rights are mythical and are really fake or met-

1   Rothbard, Murray N., *For a New Liberty*, Macmillan, 1973, p. 25.
2   Cooney, Ronald, "Natural Rights," *The Freeman*, October 1972, p. 628.
3   Szasz, Thomas, *The Myth of Psychotherapy*, Anchor, 1979, p. xv.

aphorical rights. By the same token, I say that natural law is mythical and is really fake or metaphorical law.

The metaphorical nature of natural rights is obvious in many statements by natural rights mythologizers. Consider a few examples. According to Ronald Dworkin, "Individual rights are political trumps held by individuals."[4] But will Dworkin's individual rights *literally* trump the guns held by a bunch of cops enforcing an "unjust" law? Can shrimps whistle? John Hospers writes, "And so I put up a 'no trespassing' sign, which marks off the area of my right. Each individual's right is his 'no trespassing' sign in relation to me and others."[5] Of course, unlike a real, literal "no trespassing" sign, natural rights are invisible. But what use is an invisible "no trespassing" sign? Another natural rights mythologizer is Eric Mack, who says, "Lockean rights alone provide the moral philosophical barrier against the State's encroachment upon Society."[6] But a "moral philosophical barrier" is merely a metaphorical barrier, and it will no more prevent the state's encroachment upon "Society" than a moral philosophical shield will stop an arrow from piercing your body.

But if natural rights are merely fake or metaphorical rights, what then are real rights? Real rights are those rights actually conferred and enforced by the laws of a state or the customs of a social group.

4   Dworkin, Ronald, *Taking Rights Seriously*, Harvard University, 1978, p. xi.
5   Hospers, John, *Libertarianism*, Reason Press, 1972, p. 58.
6   Mack, Eric, "Society's Foe," *Reason*, September 1976, p. 35.

Such rights are sometimes called "positive rights." As Maurice Cranston puts it, "Positive rights are facts. They are what men actually have."[7] In short, positive rights are actual, factual rights. Natural rights, by contrast, are rights that supposedly "ought" to be conferred and enforced by law or custom, rights that people supposedly "ought" to have. But, as Jeremy Bentham said, "Right is the child of law; from real laws come real rights, but from imaginary laws, from the 'laws of nature'...come imaginary rights."[8] Thus, natural rights are imaginary rights.

In my view, natural law and natural rights are human *inventions* (not *discoveries*) intended to further the interests of the inventors. As Laurence Labadie put it, "all theories of 'rights' are merely human inventions, used by one party or another in order to enhance, as they think, their ability in getting along in the world."[9] It is misleading, therefore, to contrast natural law with man-made law, for natural law is just as surely man-made as any governmental law. The difference is that laws made by government are enforced by the punishment of detected violators by the government, while natural laws are not enforced by the punishment of violators by nature. Ironically, this latter point is well made by Robert LeFevre in his essay "Moral Law," wherein he explains that he is

7   Cranston, Maurice, "What are Human Rights?," *The Human Rights Reader*, edited by Walter Laqueur and Barry Rubin, New American Library, 1979, p. 17.
8   Bentham, Jeremy, *Anarchical Fallacies*, quoted in Maurice Cranston, *op. cit.*, p. 18.
9   Labadie, Laurence, *Selected Essays*, Ralph Myles, 1978, p. 48.

"looking for a natural law." LeFevre writes,

> Here is a man who spends his life cheating, stealing and robbing others. Is there something in nature which decrees that sooner or later he will suffer for his negative and unwanted actions? Studies indicate that there is no natural retaliation. While it may be true that some thieves will suffer; it is equally true that some will not. The miscreant has to protect himself from his outraged neighbors who know of his excesses, but the rain and the sun treat him the same way they treat others. All the laws of nature behave toward the thief exactly as they behave toward his victim.[10]

By contrast, Samuel Edward Konkin III will not concede this truth, and, so he pompously pontificates,

> LeFevre chooses to look at the world from the irrational eyes of the aggressor who wishes to initiate his action and be free of its consequences. I have no intention of faking reality for the violence-initiators. Perhaps he can evade apprehension for his theft or blow as one who jumps [off] a cliff can be wafted away on a strong updraft; but the natural consequence of gravity is falling to one's death and the natural consequence of invasion is restoration.[11]

10   LeFevre, Robert, "Moral Law," *Rampart Individualist*, Vol. 1, No. 3, p. 15.

11   Konkin, Samuel Edward, III, "Reply to LeFevre," *Strategy of the New Libertarian Alliance*," No. 1, p. 28.

Konkin says he has no intention of faking reality, but it looks more like he has no intention of *facing* reality. I have never jumped off a cliff precisely because my experience with jumps from lesser heights leads me to agree that the natural consequence of jumping off a cliff (without something like a hang-glider to break one's descent) is death or at least serious injury. However, I have plenty of experience with "invasion," both as an invad*er* and an invad*ee*. And I know from that experience that "restoration" is *not* the natural consequence of "invasion." It was over ten years ago that my cassette recorder with built-in AM/FM radio was stolen from my car, which I had foolishly left unlocked while parked in a college parking lot. Under the circumstances, I had not the faintest clue as to who might have stolen it and, thus, no means of getting them to return it. It has not been returned to me to this day. I repeat: Restoration is *not* the natural consequence of invasion. Natural law is *not* enforced by nature.

Since the many different inventors of natural laws and natural rights have had different interests to further, it is not surprising that they have invented a wide variety of different and conflicting natural laws and natural rights. As George H. Smith has written, "In its various manifestations throughout history, natural law theory has been used to justify oligarchy, feudalism, theocracy, and even socialism."[12] Aristotle, for example, held that some men are slaves "by na-

---

12   Smith, George H., review of *Natural Law in Political Thought* by Paul E. Sigmund, *Libertarian Review*, December 1974, p. 1.

ture."[13] But Etienne de la Boetie claimed that "we are all naturally free."[14] Concerning "the doctrine that every man has a natural right to certain freedoms simply because he is a man," Alisdair Macintyre writes, "Diggers and Levellers gave different interpretations to this doctrine at the economic level; the Diggers believed in community of goods, and especially in common ownership of land, the Levellers in private property."[15] According to Russell Kirk, Hugo Grotius "had argued that one of the laws of nature is this: that a conqueror has the right to slaughter or perpetually enslave a whole people whose armies he has defeated."[16] But Montesquieu said this would deny the natural law of preservation of life.[17] John Locke asserted that there is a natural right to punish violators of the natural law.[18] Herbert Morris has gone so far as to claim that such violators themselves have a right to be punished![19] But Robert LeFevre asserts that to coercively punish a violator of rights is simply to violate the "inalienable rights" of the rights-violator. In 1796, followers of Babeuf, the French egalitarian and communist, proclaimed, "Nature has given every

13   Meltzer, Milton, *Slavery*, Dell, 1877, p. 55.
14   Boetie, Etienne de la, *The Politics of Obedience: The Discourse of Voluntary Servitude*, Free Life, 1975, pp. 56–57.
15   Macintyre, Alisdair, *A Short History of Ethics*, Macmillan, 1966, p. 135.
16   Kirk, Russell, *The Roots of American Order*, Open Court, 1978, p. 353.
17   *Ibid.*
18   Locke, John, *The Second Treatise of Government*, Bobbs-Merrill, 1952, p. 6.
19   Machan, Tibor R., *A Rationale for Human Rights Theory*, unpublished doctoral dissertation, p. 146.

man an equal right to the enjoyment of its goods."[20] But this, of course, is contradicted by anti-egalitarian exponents of the natural rights myth. Mortimer Adler asserts that "our primary natural right is the right to the pursuit of happiness."[21] From this, he then derives various "subsidiary natural rights—rights to life, security of life and limb, a decent livelihood, freedom from coercion, political liberty, educational opportunities, medical care, sufficient free time for the pursuits of leisure, and so on..."[22] But many libertarian exponents of natural rights would reject at least four of the eight "subsidiary natural rights" listed by Adler. According to Jeffrey Paul, Alan Gewirth "defends redistribution [of property] as the appropriate means to protect the right to well-being," but this displeases the libertarian Paul, who sees this as conflicting with his own cherished "property rights."[23] Even Adolf Hitler appealed to "the eternal law of nature" to justify the enslavement of Slavs:

> It is the eternal law of nature that gives Germany as the stronger power the right before history to subjugate these peoples of inferior race, to dominate them and to coerce them into performing

20   Babouvists, the, "Analysis of the Doctrine of Babeuf," *Socialist Thought*, edited by Albert Fried and Ronald Sanders, Anchor, 1964, p. 55.

21   Adler, Mortimer, *The Time of Our Lives*, Holt, Rinehart and Winston, 1970, p. 143.

22   *Ibid.*

23   Paul, Jeffrey, "Resurrecting Rights," *Reason*, December 1979, p. 37.

useful labors. I admit this has nothing to do with Christian ethics, but the very fact that it is according to the more ancient and well-tried laws of nature makes it the more likely to last a long while.[24]

Thus as George Smith has written,

When libertarians claim that coercion is contrary to natural law (or the nature of man), they must realize that, aside from the truth or falsity of this assertion, such an appeal to 'nature' places them in a confused and nebulous political tradition.[25]

Confused and nebulous indeed.

24 Irving, David, *Hitler's War*, Viking, 1977, p. 315.
25 Smith, *loc. cit.*

As I'VE SAID, NATURAL LAWS and natural rights are inventions intended to advance the interests of the inventors (whom I shall call "natural legislators"). What is often involved is an attempt to manipulate other people into behaving as desired by a natural legislator by duping them into accepting the values of the natural legislator as the values of nature. Thus, the personal, subjective preferences of a natural legislator are passed off as the impersonal, objective requirements of nature. For example, Frederick D. Wilhelmsen writes that

> Natural law insists that pornography...is bad and that it is bad not just for me, but for everybody, and it equally insists that not only must I not

invade my neighbor's property but that he must not invade mine or anybody else's.[26]

In other words, *Frederick Wilhelmsen* insists that pornography is bad for everybody, and *he* equally insists that no one must invade anybody else's property. But in order to give his personal preferences greater authority, Wilhelmsen pretends that it is nature who is doing all the insisting.

Related to the myth of natural rights is the myth of duty.

As John Hospers explains,

> We speak of "natural rights" or "human rights"— rights that human beings have "because of their very nature as human beings": for example, the right to life, the right to liberty and the pursuit of happiness. What specifically do these rights involve?
>
> ...When a man claims that he has a certain right, he is making a large claim: for there is a logical relation between the rights of A and the duties of others (B, C, D, etc.) and, similarly, if B has a right, then A, C, D, etc. have a duty. If A has a right to something, then others have a duty not to behave in such a way as to violate that right.[27]

So one person's (natural) right is everyone else's

26 Wilhelmsen, Frederick D., ed., *Christianity and Political Philosophy*, University of Georgia, 1978, p. 176.

27 Hospers, *op. cit.*, p. 50.

duty. But what is this thing called "duty"? Otto F. Kraushaar defines duty as "Whatever is necessary or required, or whatever one is morally obliged to do, as opposed to what one may be pleased or inclined to do."[28] According to Ayn Rand, "The meaning of the term duty is: the moral necessity to perform certain actions for no other reason than obedience to some higher authority, without regard to any personal goal, motive, desire or interest."[29] Or, as P.H. Nowell-Smith puts it, "The language of 'You ought' and particularly of 'duty' is frequently used in cases where the agent has no reason for doing what he is told other than the fact that it is his duty."[30]

However, Nowell-Smith gives the game away when he goes on to say, "The connexion between duties and the demands of others comes out clearly in the fact that we use the word 'obligation' as a synonym for 'duty'; and this word is derived from a root meaning 'tied,' an obvious metaphor for coercion."[31] Thus, duty is a matter of metaphorical or fake coercion. If you want someone to do something that he has no personal reason to do, but you are unable or unwilling (perhaps afraid) to use real coercion to get him to do it, then you can try to get him to do it by means of the metaphorical or fake coercion of duty. Or, as John Badcock put it, "Given a believer in duty,

28   Runes, Dagobert D., ed., *Dictionary of Philosophy*, Littlefield, Adams, 1971, p. 85.
29   Rand, Ayn, "Causality Versus Duty," *The Objectivist*, July 1970, p. 1.
30   Nowell-Smith, P.H., *Ethics*, Penguin, 1954, p. 200.
31   *Ibid.*

it becomes possible for him to be enslaved with his own consent."[32]

But, as Ayn Rand has pointed out, "Reality confronts a man with a great many 'musts,' but all of them are conditional. The formula of realistic necessity is: 'You must, if'— and the 'if' stands for man's choice; '— if you want to achieve a certain goal.' "[33] In the terminology of Immanuel Kant, such a conditional "must" is a hypothetical imperative; for example, "if you want to be happy for the rest of your life, never make a pretty woman your wife."

There are no unconditional "musts" or "oughts," no categorical imperatives (to again use Kantian phrasing). That is why, although I am an egoist of sorts, I nevertheless reject what Brian Medlin calls the principle of "universal categorical egoism," to wit, "that we all ought to observe our own interests, *because that is what we ought to do*."[34] I say, to the contrary, that it is up to each individual, insofar as he has freedom of choice in the matter, to decide for himself whether or not to pursue his own interests.

If there are no unconditional "musts" or "oughts," then there are no "duties" or "moral obligations." Which means there is no "morality," no "system of the principles and duties of right and wrong conduct."[35]

32   Badcock, John, *Slaves to Duty*, Laurence Labadie edition, n.d., p. 35.

33   Rand, *op. cit.*, p. 4.

34   Medlin, Brian, "Ultimate Principles of Ethical Egoism," *Morality and Rational Self-Interest*, edited by David P. Gauthier, Prentice Hall, 1970, p. 58.

35   *The Reader's Digest Great Encyclopedic Dictionary*, Reader's Di-

Morality (like natural law and natural rights, which are specific examples of "moral" ideas) is a myth invented to promote the interests/desires/purposes of the inventors. Morality is a device for controlling the gullible with words. "You 'must not' commit murder!" Why not? "Because murder is 'wrong!' Murder is 'immoral!'" Bunk! Murder may be impractical or excessively risky or just not worth the trouble. There are all sorts of reasons why I might refrain from committing murder, even if I would like to do so. But murder is not "wrong." Murder is not "immoral." And the same goes for rape, robbery, assault, battery, burglary, buggery, bestiality, incest, treason, torturing children, suicide, cannibalism, cannabisism, etc. Moralist Allen Wheelis says, "Morality is a wall. On it is written: Whatever passion impel you, whatever goal you pursue, beyond this limit you may not go."[36] But if morality is a wall, it is a metaphorical or fake wall, a wall built with words, not bricks, a wall that will not stop us amoralists. So if you want to be safe from us, Allen Wheelis, you'd better build some *real* walls.

I've said that morality is a myth and have dubbed myself an "amoralist." But according to moralist Tibor R. Machan, "all people *must* play the moral game." Why? Machan writes,

> This we see by noting that it is perfectly natural to ask questions pertaining to the moral worthiness of people in *any* circumstances, provided

gest Association, 1968, p. 880.
36   Wheelis, Allen, *The Moralist*, Penguin, 1973, p. 74.

they are capable of thinking for themselves and choosing between various alternative ways of thinking and acting. Such notions that someone *ought to have* done otherwise than he did, that we should have behaved differently from how we did behave, or that we should do this or that when we get into this or that situation—all these are tied to our human way of life. It is our way of life which attests to the necessity of morality.[37]

It may be "perfectly natural" for Machan, a moralist, to ask questions about the "moral worthiness" of people, but why is it *necessary* for all people to ask such questions?

Machan says that various kinds of moral discourse "are thoroughly tied to our human way of life" and that "it is our way of life which attests to the necessity of morality." But while I would grant that "our human way of life" makes it *possible* for people to play the "moral game," Machan has not explained why or proven that we all "*must*" play the "moral game."

There are those who agree with me that there are no unconditional musts or oughts but who nevertheless write about something they call morality. For example, George H. Smith has written about something he calls "rational morality," as distinguished from "religious morality." But Smith's "rational morality" is based on *positing* happiness as "man's ultimate value." And Smith himself says,

37   Machan, Tibor R., "A Rationale for Human Rights," *The Personalist*, Spring 1971, p. 228.

> I will not argue that all men actually pursue happiness, nor that all men 'ought' to pursue happiness (whatever such an assertion might mean); rather, I shall offer happiness as a hypothetical goal. In other words, *if* a man desires happiness, *then* he ought to be concerned with those conditions, those values, that are conducive to man's happiness.[38]

Smith's "rational morality," to paraphrase Harry Browne, is neither an absolute nor a universal morality; it is merely a personal morality. It is binding or obligatory only on those who, like Smith presumably, pursue happiness as their ultimate value. Of course, many people pursue other values as their ultimate value, such as survival, or autonomy, or family, or duty. And whatever one posits as one's ultimate value, there will be certain subsidiary values deemed conducive to the achievement of that ultimate value. I wonder why it is only the pursuit of happiness as an ultimate value that provides a basis for "*rational morality*"? Is it, for example, *irrational* to pursue personal autonomy as one's highest value? In any case, I want to emphasize that Smith's "rational morality" is not morality in the sense in which I (and, I think, most people) use the term since his "rational morality" does not involve any element of duty or unconditional obligation.

As I've already said, to claim a natural right for

38   Smith, George, *Atheism: The Case Against God*, Nash, 1974, p. 228.

yourself is to assert a corresponding duty for others, to wit, the duty to refrain from acting contrary to your natural right. If, for example, you claim a natural right to life, then you also assert that I have a duty to refrain from murdering you, regardless of what my personal goals, motives, desires, or interests might be. No matter how much I might gain from murdering you, I "must not" murder you. Why not? Simply because I "must not." This "must not" is unconditional and absolute. But, as such, it is merely an arbitrary, unprovable assumption. As James J. Martin makes clear,

> Since it has no anatomical locus (nobody really knows where your natural rights are like they know, for instance, where your pancreas is), [the idea of natural rights] involves an ability to deal with intangible things of this sort. They amount to matters that have no dimensions and I call them religious ideas—there is no challenging them. Someone who supports a religious idea involving the Trinity or Transubstantiation or a number of other religious doctrines is irrefutable. There is no way of proving these things and there's no way of disproving them. If someone wishes to maintain that he has these intangible things called rights, well, what is one to say about it? You can't disprove it—but again there's no way of proving them either.[39]

39 Martin, James J., "Introducing Revisionism: An Interview With James J. Martin," *Reason*, Janurary 1976, p. 19.

As a matter of fact, some devotees of the myth of natural rights admit that their claims about natural rights are simply unproven assumptions. For example, Ronald Dworkin, sympathetically explicating the views of John Rawls, writes that "justice as fairness rests on the assumption of a natural right of all men and women to equality of concern and respect, a right they possess not by virtue of birth or characteristic or merit or excellence but simply as human beings with the capacity to make plans and give justice."[40] But some natural rights mythologizers seem to think that their belief in natural rights is something more than an unprovable assumption. They have presented arguments that purport to rationally demonstrate the reality of natural rights. In the remaining chapters, I'm going to examine some such arguments to see if they demonstrate anything beyond the wishful thinking and faulty logic of the exponents of the myth.

40   Dworkin, *op. cit.*, p. 4.

IRONICALLY, AYN RAND, who debunked the myth of "duty" by pointing out that in reality all "musts" are conditional, was nevertheless an influential exponent of the myth of natural rights. In an essay on "Man's Rights," Rand wrote as follows:

> The concept of individual rights is so new in human history that most men have not grasped it fully to this day. In accordance with the two theories of ethics, the mystical or the social, some men assert that rights are a gift of God—others, that rights are a gift of society. But, in fact, the source of man's rights is man's nature.
>
> The Declaration of Independence stated that men "are endowed by their Creator with certain unalienable rights." Whether one believes that

man is the product of a Creator or of nature, the issue of man's origin does not alter the fact that he is an entity of a specific kind—a rational being—that he cannot function successfully under coercion, and that rights are a necessary condition of his particular mode of survival.

"The source of man's rights is not divine law or congressional law, but the law of identity. A is A—and Man is Man. *Rights* are conditions of existence required by man's nature for his proper survival. If man is to live on earth, it is *right* for him to use his mind, it is *right* to act on his own free judgment, it is *right* to work for his own values and keep the product of his work. If life on this earth is his purpose, he has a *right* to live as a rational being; nature forbids him the irrational." (*Atlas Shrugged*)[41]

According to Rand, rights are a necessary condition of "man's" particular mode of survival. This ties in with her assertion that "man" is "an entity of a specific kind—a rational being" and "cannot function successfully under coercion." But, while there is *some* truth in the claim that "man" cannot function successfully under coercion, the claim is nevertheless far from being a universal truth. Obviously, few people are able to function successfully under coercion in the form of a bullet fired into their brain without their consent. And there are, of

41   Rand, Ayn, *The Virtue of Selfishness*, New American Library, pp. 94–95.

course, other forms of coercion that might impair to some degree a person's ability to function successfully. But some of the less drastic forms of coercion, though inconvenient to the coercee, are not necessarily incompatible with his functioning successfully. Consider: All of us who live in state-dominated societies and who are not members or beneficiaries of the state apparatus are living under some degree of coercion, if only by dint of being forced to pay taxes. Yet, despite living under state coercion, many people still manage to function successfully. Ayn Rand herself provided a good example of someone who was able to function successfully despite living under coercion by the state.

As Albert Ellis has written,

> Because a man is supposedly a rational being, Miss Rand *assumes* that he cannot function successfully under coercion. Actually, the more rational he is *the more* successfully he can function under almost any conditions, including coercion. It is fairly obvious that he can function *better* without than with coercion; but even this is not always true. Children often function better with some degree of forced discipline or coercion; and hordes of so-called adults, too! Even if man does get along better without coercion, individual rights that preclude his being too coerced socially are hardly a *necessary* condition of his particular mode of survival. We know that he survives without such individual rights; we can only say that

> he usually survives *better* or *more happily* with them.[42]

Furthermore, insofar as it *is* true that "man" cannot function successfully under coercion, it *is* also true that *animals* cannot function successfully under coercion. Being shot in the head is just as detrimental to the successful functioning of a deer as it is to the successful functioning of a "man." Therefore, if a "right" to freedom from coercion is a necessary condition of "man's" particular mode of survival, then a "right" to freedom from coercion is also a necessary condition of a deer's particular mode of survival. And, by the same token, a "right" to freedom from coercion must also be a necessary condition of every animal's and plant's particular mode of survival, inasmuch as every animal and plant is vulnerable to being injured or killed by coercive action.

Although his views may no longer be the same, George Smith made essentially the same point in his essay "Ayn Rand and the Right to Life: A Critical Evaluation." Smith writes,

> it should be apparent that Rand's prerequisite for the right to life is equally applicable to any life form. A steer "cannot function successfully under coercion" either; a steer being led to slaughter requires the recognition of his means of survival *if* he is to continue living; "rights are a necessary condition of his particular mode of survival" as

42   Ellis, Albert, *Is Objectivism a Religion?*, Lyle Stuart, 1968, p. 146.

well. If the steer is to survive, the creatures capable of moral action—the creatures capable of recognizing an obligation—must recognize the steer's "right" to his own life.

If the metaphysical requirements of an organism's survival (concerning its relationship with volitional creatures) constitutes a *criterion* for the possession of the right to life sanction, then this moral sanction must properly apply to all life, insofar as these organisms enter into relationships with men.

Ultimately, Rand's only possible source for her right to life is a moral sanction on the process *as such*, life as the ultimate value of each individual organism. This would mean that moral creatures (men) are obligated not to interfere *via* the initiation of force with the life processes of all other organisms (including other men); to do so would be a violation of a right and, hence, immoral. *Man's* right to life, then, would be merely a specific application of the general life sanction.[43]

But if all living things possess a "right" to life, what then?

Smith spells out the enormously significant implications as follows:

My argument is this: Ayn Rand's derivation of man's inalienable right to his own life rests *im-*

43   Smith, George H., "Ayn Rand and the Right to Life: A Critical Evaluation," *Invictus* 17, p. 8.

plicitly on a moral sanction of life *as such*; and, if she is to be at all consistent, Rand must apply her rights concept to all life forms. A sanction on all life, however, is inconsistent with man's survival. To live, man must kill other life—he cannot survive on inorganic matter. To posit that every living organism has a "right to life" results in the absurd situation that man, in order to be "moral" (i.e., in order not to violate any rights), must sacrifice his own life. The mere sustaining of man's life would necessarily entail immoral action on his part. Taken to its logical consequences, then, Rand's use of the right to life proves to be diametrically opposed to her philosophical egoism.[44]

Thus, Rand's argument for "man's rights" is self defeating. "Man" has a "right to life." But if "man" has a right to life, then so does every living thing. And, in that case, "man" cannot "morally" survive. To be "moral," he must not sustain his life since that means violating the "right to life" of some other organism. Ironically, therefore, "man's *right* to life" is inimical to "man's" *life*.

The source of this paradox is that Rand based "man's rights" on what "man" *needs* for survival. "Rights," as Rand put it, "are a necessary condition of man's particular mode of survival." But for every form of life, there are necessary conditions (needs) for its particular mode of survival, Rand's argument implies that every form of life has rights.

44   Smith, *op. cit.*, p. 4.

But, as Rand herself sometimes said, *need is not a claim*. "Man's" need of freedom from coercion, for example, does not constitute a claim or a right to such freedom any more than "man's" need of food constitutes a claim or right to food. Those who believe that "man's" need of food does constitute a claim or right to food, and who believe that the government must guarantee that "man" has food, are sometimes known as "bleeding-heart liberals." By the same token, those who believe that "man's" need of freedom from coercion constitutes a claim or right to freedom from coercion, and who believe that the government must guarantee that "man" has freedom from coercion, could be called "bleeding-heart libertarians."

There is another aspect of Rand's argument for "man's rights" which is open to criticism. Consider this passage:

> If a man is to live on earth, it is *right* for him to use his mind, it is *right* for him to act on his own judgment, it is *right* to work for his values and to keep the product of his work. If life on earth is his purpose, he has a *right* to live as a rational being; nature forbids him the irrational.

As John W. Robbins has pointed out,

> The first three times the word 'right' is used, it appears as an adjective modifying an action; at the last it appears as a noun, denoting the attribute of a person. The connection between the two con-

cepts is not mentioned but the reader is expected to believe there is one, for no better reason than that the two words are spelled and pronounced alike.[45]

To argue that because it *is right* for "man" to act on his own free judgment, he therefore *has a right* to do so is similar to arguing that because my chest *is cold*, I therefore *have a cold* in my chest. To establish that something *is right* for "man" simply does not imply that "man" *has a right* to it.

But what is all this talk about "man"? "Man," after all, is only an abstraction and is not a real, living being. It is only *men* (that is, people) who live, not "man." And men are all unique individuals, with unique physiognomies, temperaments, metabolisms, body chemistries, personalities, mentalities, tastes, preferences, prejudices, talents, aptitudes, abilities, beliefs, desires, interests, values, and purposes. By talking about "man" and what is right for "man," Rand obscures the fact that what is right for one man may conflict with what is right for another man. While it may be right for one man to act on his own free judgment, it may also be right for another man to act on his own free judgment to prevent the first man from doing so. Such conflicts between what is right for one man and what is right for another man mean that it is absurd to assert that all men have a right to what is right for them.

45   Robbins, John W., *Answer to Ayn Rand*, self-published, 1974, p. 118.

Max Stirner said, "He who is infatuated with *Man* leaves persons out of account so far as that infatuation exists, and floats in an ideal, sacred interest. *Man,* you see, is not a person, but an ideal, a spook."[46] Rand was infatuated with "man", and, as Stirner said, she floated "in an ideal, sacred interest." As George Smith pointed out, Rand's arguments for "man's" right to life rested on a "moral sanction" on "man's life." In other words, Rand believed that "man's life" is sacred. Rand never said this in so many words (though one of her followers, Stanley Lieberman, has done so[47]), but she came very close to saying it in her introduction to the 25th anniversary edition of *The Fountainhead.* There, Rand complained that such concepts as "exaltation," "worship," "reverence, " and "sacred" have been monopolized by religion. "But," she said, "such concepts do name actual emotions even though no supernatural dimension exists."[48] So, she continued, "It is the highest level of man's emotions that has to be redeemed from the muck of mysticism and redirected at its proper object: man."[49] She then identified the "sense of life" dramatized in *The Fountainhead* as "man worship." As Max Stirner observed, "Our atheists are pious people."[50]

46   Stirner, Max, *The Ego and His Own*, Libertarian Book Club, 1963, p. 79.

47   Lieberman, Stanley, "Certain Unalienable Rights," *A is A Newsletter*, May 1972, p. 4.

48   Rand, Ayn, *The Fountainhead*, New American Library, 1968, p. ix.

49   *Ibid.*

50   Stirner, *op. cit.*

Rand, it seems, considered "man" and "man's life" to be sacred. But I say; Nothing is sacred. Nothing is "entitled to reverence." Nothing is "inviolable." However, Daniel C. Maguire insists that

> The notion of sacredness is more basic than the notion of God. Even those who dispense with the idea of God must deal with the sacred…It is a functioning category of human existence without which the human animal cannot be understood. If nothing is sacred, human life becomes absurd, and ethical discourse is rendered inane.[51]

But, contrary to Maguire, "the sacred" is a category necessary to the understanding only of *some* human animals, specifically those two-legged sheep who believe in "the sacred." Maguire says that "If nothing is sacred, human life becomes absurd, and ethical discourse is rendered inane." But so what? If human life *is* absurd and ethical discourse *is* inane, then so be it. Apparently, Maguire cannot face the possibility that that's the way it is, and so he clings to "the sacred", like Linus clutching his security blanket. Max Stirner said, "Everything sacred is a tie, a fetter."[52] But, fortunately for us amoralistic egoists, "the sacred" is only a metaphorical tie, a metaphorical fetter, and can restrain only those who, like Maguire, choose to be bound and shackled by it.

According to Rand, "If life on earth is his purpose,

51   Maguire, Daniel C., *The Moral Choice*, Doubleday, 1978, p. 73.
52   Stirner, *op. cit.*

he [man] has a *right* to live as a rational being; nature forbids him the irrational." Rand took the truth that irrationality *can* be incompatible with living on Earth and, by means of typically Randian overgeneralization, turned it into a falsehood. In fact, nature "permits" a helluva lot of irrationality. How, for example, could Christianity have survived for nearly two millennia if nature "forbids" the irrational? How could maniacs like Jack Van Impe, Tim LaHaye, and Pastor John Hagee survive and even prosper if nature "forbids" the irrational? For that matter, considering the irrational aspects of her own philosophy, such as her doctrine of "man's rights," how was it possible for Rand to live such a long and successful life if nature "forbids" the irrational?

Nathaniel Branden, who for years was designated by Rand as her "intellectual heir," once dubbed her "Mrs. Logic"; but whatever else may have justified this appellation, the fact remains that when Rand argued for "man's rights," she was not "Mrs. Logic": she was "Mrs. *Illogic*."

ANOTHER EXPONENT OF THE NATURAL-RIGHTS myth is the Rand-influenced philosopher Tibor R. Machan, aka "Mr. Morality." Whereas Rand wrote about "man's rights," Machan writes about "human rights." But Machan's "human rights" are also "natural rights" since they supposedly derive from "human nature," specifically from the interrelated human traits of rationality (the capacity to think conceptually) and freedom (the capacity to choose whether or not to think conceptually).

According to Machan, a "morally good" person is one who is "fully aware."[53] Or, as he also puts it, "moral perfection amounts, in the final analysis, to a person's being as fully conceptually aware as his

53   Machan, Tibor R., *A Rationale for Human Rights Theory*, unpublished doctoral dissertation, p. 146.

capacities allow him to be."[54] Or, as he also says, "basic virtue (being morally good) consists in living by the exercise of one's mind to the highest potential."[55] This is all somewhat vague, whether Machan is taking about being as fully aware as possible or about using one's mind to the highest potential. But things get a bit confused when it turns out that using one's mind to its *fullest* capacity is not the same thing as using it to its *highest* capacity. Machan says, "Thus, for instance, a philosopher is at his moral best when he exercises his mind to ITS FULLEST (not just highest) capacity on his particular level AS man AND philosopher."[56] Machan gives not the faintest clue as to what the difference is between using one's mind to its fullest capacity and using it to its highest capacity. But, for some unspecified reason, he thinks the former is better than the latter. (Was Machan at his "moral best," using his mind to its fullest capacity, when he wrote his doctoral dissertation, from which I am quoting?)

In any case, having set up this nebulous criterion of "morality," Machan proceeds to derive the "human right to liberty" as follows:

> Human rights pertain to what claims men have made vis-à-vis each other and how we are to judge between them. The connection between what a human right is and a conception of a good human

---

54   Machan, *op. cit.*, p. 126.
55   Machan, *op. cit.*, p. 129.
56   Machan, *op. cit.*, pp. 130–131.

life may be conceived as follows: What is morally right for a human being as an individual (what he should do) relates to what is good for him within OR outside a human community. In this sense, the "good" and "right" of political conditions are prudential, utilitarian: they are good and right because they serve the purpose of making a morally good life possible for people. (Without the right to be free, for instance, and, thus, in a condition of coercion, it would be impossible to be either good or bad; one would have no chance for freedom of action, that is, to be an agent, to produce or do what is good or evil.) Depending on the context, what is morally appropriate will emerge. Thus, if a good human life is indeed a life guided by a fullest degree of awareness, then within the context of society this condition would have to be sought after. What, in short, can secure the social conditions right for man to fulfill his moral purpose, his utmost degree of human awareness, his fullest degree of humanity? What social conditions facilitate and enable the moral growth of individual human beings?

We have seen that a man's moral goodness depends on whether he chooses to be as fully aware as possible to him. In order for man to reach HIS highest level of awareness and act on it, he must be free to judge and to act on his judgments. This is true for EVERY man...If interference upon this freedom occurs, the person who has been interfered with has been robbed of his opportunity and responsibility as a moral agent; if his judgment has been inhibited, his actions interfered with, he cannot be considered fully free and responsible. And this again is true of all men, all to whom human rights must be accorded. Thus, it is not necessary to specify that human freedom is LIMITED by the rights of other persons. If all men are to be free to judge and act upon their judgments, that already tells us that such action cannot involve interference with others' freedom.

The human right which emerges from this analysis is the right to be free. Of course it is a right which arises out of the moral value of individual human life and of free judgment and action. Political liberty, for this is what we are talking about, is based on the legal implementation of human rights, on the implicit or explicit recognition by all of a given community of men that each man's life is of supreme value and that a human life requires freedom of judgment and action to develop morally.[57]

(Notice that Machan, having previously distinguished between using one's mind to its fullest potential and using it to its highest potential, now, in the first two sentences of the second paragraph of the above-quoted passage, treats these as being equivalent. Obviously, whatever Machan's criterion of "morality" amounts to, it is no more clear to Machan than it is to me.)

57   Machan, *op. cit.*, pp. 132-133.

Machan begins by asserting that "moral goodness" depends on whether or not a person chooses to be as fully aware as possible. But then, without explanation, he changes this to make "moral goodness" contingent upon a person's being as fully aware as possible and acting on that awareness. Thus, he says,

> Without the right to be free, for instance, and, thus, in a condition of coercion, it would be impossible to be either good or bad; one would have no chance for freedom of action, that is, to be an agent, to produce or do what is either good or evil.

But Machan simply contradicts himself when he makes a person's "moral goodness" depend on whether or not other people coerce him and thereby restrict his freedom of action. Previously Machan asserted that

> the most important act for purposes of moral philosophy, the act for which all men can be held responsible if they fail to perform it because it lies at the base of all other acts and is itself undetermined FOR US but determined BY US to be or not to be performed, is the act of conceptual consciousness, the act to think.[58]

And, according to Machan, man, by his very nature, possesses the freedom to choose to think or to not think. So even if a man's external freedom of ac-

58   Machan, *op. cit.*, p. 123.

tion is limited by coercion, he still retains his internal freedom to choose to think or to not think and can be judged accordingly. Thus, there is no reason whatever for Machan's assertion that being in a condition of coercion makes it impossible for a person to be either "good" or "bad." A person in a condition of coercion can still be "morally good" in Machan's sense of being "as fully aware as possible." Thus, Machan's own premises negate his conclusion that a "right to be free" is a necessary condition for men to be "morally good" in a social context.

But even if one accepted the notion that being "morally good" depends upon being as fully aware as possible *and* acting on the basis of that awareness, this might, at best, prove the necessity of a rather limited degree of political freedom. As long as a person is not totally deprived of freedom of action—for example, by being bound hand-and-foot—then, even in a state of coercion, he can think and judge and act on his judgments. Even if the government prohibits some activity, such as publicly criticizing the government, and threatens to punish those who violate the prohibition, an individual can still think about and judge the government's prohibition and can, on the basis of his thinking and judging, determine whether or not to obey that prohibition. So Machan's criterion of "morality" would still be applicable even in a condition of coercion, and, thus, Machan has not proven that a "right to be free" is necessary for people to be able to be "morally good."

But even if Machan had proven this point, another question would arise: Why is Machan concerned with whether or not *other people* are able to live "morally good" lives? Why does he want *all* men to be free to judge and act on their judgments? Machan says that "each man's life is of supreme value," but what does this mean? To *whom* is each man's life of supreme value? To himself? To everybody? To Machan? My life is of supreme value to me; Machan's life is not. Even if I wanted to live a "morally good" life (in Machan's sense), why would I (or "should" I) care whether or not *Machan* is able to live such a "morally good" life? I'd like to see how Machan, the ostensible egoist, answers that question.

Machan's doctoral dissertation is entitled *A Rationale for Human Rights Theory*. But, considering my above-stated criticisms of it, I think a better title would be *A Rationalization for Human Rights Theory*.

A LEADING CONTEMPORARY EXPONENT of the myth of natural rights is Murray N. Rothbard. Rothbard's political creed is based on the "axiom" (i.e., dogma) of "nonaggression against anyone's person and property."[59] Rothbard finds a foundation for this axiom in "natural rights." Here is part of Rothbard's argument:

> Let us turn to the natural-rights basis for the libertarian creed, a basis which, in one form or another, has been adopted by most of the libertarians, past and present. "Natural rights" is the cornerstone of a political philosophy which, in turn, is embedded in a greater structure of "natural law." Natural law theory rests on the insight

59 Rothbard, Murray N., *For A New Liberty*, Macmillan, 1973, p. 23.

that we live in a world of more than one—in fact, a vast number—of entities, and that each entity has distinct and specific properties, a distinct "nature," which can be investigated by man's reason, by his sense of perception and mental faculties. Copper has a distinct nature and behaves in a certain way, and so does iron, salt, etc. The species man, therefore, has a specifiable nature, as does the world around him and the ways of interaction between them. To put it with undue brevity, the activity of each inorganic and organic entity is determined by its own nature and by the nature of the other entities with which it comes in contact. Specifically, while the behavior of plants and at least the lower animals is determined by their biological nature or perhaps by their "instincts," the nature of man is such that each individual person must, in order to act, choose his own ends and employ his own means in order to attain them. Possessing no automatic instincts, each man must learn about himself and the world, use his mind to select values, learn about cause and effect, and act purposively to maintain himself and advance his life. Since men can think, feel, evaluate, and act only as individuals, it becomes vitally necessary for each man's survival and prosperity that he be free to learn, choose, develop his faculties, and act upon his knowledge and values. This is the necessary path of human nature; to interfere with and cripple this process by using violence goes profoundly against what

> is necessary by man's nature for his life and pros-
> perity. Violent interference with a man's learning
> and choices is therefore profoundly "antihuman,"
> it violates the natural law of man's needs.[60]

Essentially, Rothbard's argument is that each man needs to be free to learn, choose, develop his faculties and act upon his values in order to maintain and advance his life. To interfere with his process by violence goes against what is necessary by "man's" nature for his life and prosperity. "Violent interference with a man's learning and choices is therefore profoundly 'antihuman,' it violates the natural law of man's needs." But, granted that violent interference with a man's freedom generally tends to undercut his ability to live and prosper, the question is: Why should one man refrain from violently interfering with the freedom of another man simply because the other man (like all men) needs freedom? Why should I refrain from violently interfering with Murray Rothbard's freedom simply because Murray Rothbard needs freedom? If I can advance my life by violent interference with Murray Rothbard's freedom, why should I care what Murray Rothbard needs?

Rothbard says such interference is "antihuman." But, while violent interference with Murray Rothbard's freedom may be anti-Rothbardian, if it helps me, a human, advance my life, then how can it be unequivocally "antihuman"? If I violently interfere with Murray Rothbard's freedom, my action may be

60   Rothbard, *op. cit.* pp. 30–31.

contrary to Rothbard's nature, but it is not contrary to my nature.

According to John A. Goodson and David M. Longinotti,

> There are…a number of problems with the derivation of natural rights, but one is fundamental. In defining man's nature, the savage characteristics are dismissed as being not proper to man. For Ayn Rand, "man's survival *qua* man" means a rational, productive existence, and anything else is nonhuman. But to assert that a human can have characteristics that are not human is to assert that A can be not-A, thus attempting to deny the law of identity. If, as Rothbard points out, "the activity of each inorganic and organic entity is determined by its own nature," then is it not true that the *violent* activity of an organism (for example, man) is also determined by its nature? And if, as John Hospers writes in *Libertarianism*, an organism "acts for its survival by means implanted in it by nature," then must not the predatory acts of one man against another also be implanted by nature?
>
> The point is that an organism's "nature" is what it *is*, or can be. It is not within an elephant's nature to fly; it *is* within a man's nature to steal.[61]

While it is in "man's nature" to be free from vi-

61   Goodson, John A. and David M. Longinotti, "Those 'Natural' Rights Aren't," *Reason*, September, 1977, p. 35.

olent interference by other men, it is also in "man's nature" to violently interfere with the freedom of other men. Again, if I violently interfere with Murray Rothbard's freedom, this may violate the "natural law" of Murray Rothbard's needs, but it doesn't violate the "natural law" of *my* needs.

Rothbard continues his natural rights argument as follows:

> The most viable method of elaborating the natural rights statement of the libertarian position is to divide it into parts, and to begin with the basic axiom of the "right to self-ownership." The right to self-ownership asserts the absolute right of each man, by virtue of his (or her) being a human being, to "own" his or her own body; that is, to control that body free of coercive interference. Since each individual must think, learn, value, and choose his or her ends and means in order to survive and flourish, the right to self-ownership gives man the right to perform these vital activities without being hampered by coercive molestation.[62]

Rothbard's "right to self-ownership," like Rand's "right to life," is based on what men *need* to survive and flourish. But, as I've already said, *need is not a claim*. Rothbard's argument shows that he is just another bleeding-heart libertarian.

Rothbard's argument bases "human rights" on

62   Rothbard, *op. cit.*, 26–27.

human survival needs, which raises the question: Why don't the survival needs of all other organisms generate "rights" for those organisms? After all, they need freedom from violent interference with their survival activities as much as men do. Rothbard, however, clearly does not believe that animals have "rights." He says, "Animals are 'economic land,' since they are original nature-given resources."[63] And he presumably also considers plants to be "economic land." But the unanswered question is: Why aren't other men also "economic land"? Why can't (or "shouldn't") they also be viewed as "original nature-given resources"?

Rothbard's argument for the "right to self-ownership" continues:

> Consider ...the consequences of denying each man a right to his own person. There are only two alternatives: either (1) a certain class of people, A, have a right to own another class, B, or (2) everyone has the right to own his own equal quotal share of everyone else. The first alternative implies that while Class A deserves the rights of being human, Class B is in reality subhuman and therefore deserves no such rights. But since they are indeed human beings, the first alternative contradicts itself in denying natural human rights to one set of humans. Moreover, as we shall see, allowing Class A to own Class B means that the former is allowed to exploit, and

63 Rothbard, Murray N., *Egalitarianism as a Revolt Against Nature and Other Essays*, Libertarian Review Press, 1974, p. 63.

> therefore to live parasitically, at the expense of
> the latter. But this parasitism itself violates the
> basic economic requirement for life: production
> and exchange.[64]

According to Rothbard, there are only these two alternatives to his claim that each man has a "right" to his own person. But, as George I. Mavrodes has pointed out, Rothbard "neglects others that would seem initially more plausible—if for no other reason than that they have actually been practiced and recognized in the legal systems of slave-owning societies."[65] And Rothbard neglects another alternative, to wit, that nobody has any "right" to own any person. By neglecting to consider certain alternatives, Rothbard renders his arguments inconclusive at best.

But what about Rothbard's criticism of the first alternative he mentions, that a certain class of people, A, has the right to own another class, B? Rothbard says that this alternative implies that Class B is subhuman and does not deserve the rights of being human. And since they *are* human, this alternative supposedly contradicts itself in denying "human rights" to one class of humans. But this criticism rests on the unproven assumption that rights must be "human rights," deserved by all human beings or none. But suppose Class A claims their right to own Class B not on the ground that they are human beings but be-

64   Rothbard, *For A New Liberty*, p. 27.
65   Mavrodes, George I., "A Challenge to Self-Ownership," *Reason*, March 1978, p. 30.

cause they are some particular kind of human beings (members of a "superior" race, for example). In that case, the denial of rights of Class B would not imply that Class B is subhuman, only that they are not the right kind of human to deserve rights. And there is no necessary contradiction in such a claim. It may be unprovable that one kind of human being deserves rights while another kind does not. But it is no *more* unprovable than Rothbard's own position that one kind of organism (the human kind) deserves rights while other kinds do not.

Rothbard also criticizes alternative 1 on the ground that the parasitism of Class A at the expense of Class B "violates the basic economic requirement for life: production and exchange." But the basic economic requirement of life is simply the acquisition of the necessities of life by whatever means, whether by production or predation. If parasitism is incompatible with the basic economic requirement for life, then why haven't men in all slavery-based societies simply died off? Obviously, some people must produce the necessities of life if anyone is going to survive. But this doesn't imply that everyone must engage in production for everyone to survive. For example, in a slave system, the lives of both master and slave may be sustained by the productivity of the slave. Thus, parasitism can be a viable means of survival, one which is not necessarily incompatible with the survival of the victims. If there is something "wrong" with such parasitism, Rothbard hasn't proven it.

I am not going to discuss the second alternative

postulated by Rothbard, "participatory communalism," because I agree with him that it is not a practicable alternative.

Rothbard, having criticized and rejected two alternatives to his beloved "right to self-ownership," concludes by adopting as his "primary axiom" the universal "right to self-ownership." But George I. Mavrodes has made a telling point against Rothbard's argument:

> Even if we were to list every form which the ownership of human beings could possibly take and were then to find arguments ruling out all of them except self-ownership, we would still not have established the propriety of this last system. In order to justify that conclusion we should have to add still another premise to the argument— the premise that every human being is, or ought to be, owned by somebody or other. We need this premise to keep us from rejecting self-ownership right along with the other forms, concluding that human beings are not owned by anyone at all.
>
> Rothbard does not argue in this connection for the claim that everyone is owned by somebody or another. He does not even mention it. He rather seems to assume it as something so obvious that it hardly rises into consciousness at all. But is it obvious? Why should there not simply be unowned people?[66]

Rothbard's argument for the "right to self-own-

66   Mavrodes, *op. cit.*, pp. 30–31.

ership" has more holes in it than a slice of Swiss cheese and doesn't prove a damned thing.

Ironically, Rothbard himself has insisted "that it is not enough for an intellectual or social scientist to proclaim his value judgments—that these judgments must be rationally defensible and must be demonstrable to be valid, cogent and correct."[67] But, as I have shown, Rothbard fails to live up to these standards. His value judgments in favor of "self-ownership" and "nonaggression" have not been shown to be valid, cogent, and correct. And, interestingly enough, David Gordon, a sympathetic commentator on Rothbard's case for the "right to self-ownership," to whom Rothbard's argument seems "entirely convincing,"[68] nevertheless agrees with me on this point. Gordon says that to present the case in the way that Rothbard does "is in part to rely on one's moral intuitions, e.g., in seeing that slavery is wrong; and this Rothbard would see as a defect."[69] Since Rothbard's case for the "right to self-ownership" relies on his "moral intuition" or value judgment that slavery is "wrong," he has not demonstrated, but merely assumed, the correctness of his value judgments.

67   Rothbard, *Egalitarianism as a Revolt Against Nature and Other Essays*, p. 3.
68   Gordon, David, "Man vs. the State," *Inquiry*, July 1982, p. 37.
69   *Ibid.*

ANOTHER NATURAL RIGHTS MYTHOLOGIZER is Paul Lepanto, an unauthorized exponent of Ayn Rand's Objectivism, "the only rational school of contemporary philosophy."[70] Lepanto, like Rand, views "man's life" as the standard of "morality." Also like Rand, he wants to rule out certain kinds of actions that men can and do sometimes perform to sustain or enhance their lives. He tries to do so in the following passage, which essentially presents his argument for rights, though without yet using that term:

> Presumably each member of a society wishes to advance his life. What if one man (or group of men) tries to live by means of harming another man?

70   Lepanto, Paul, *Return to Reason*, Exposition Press, 1971, p. 11.

The first step in arriving at a solution to this problem is to see that such an attempt cannot be rationally justified.

Consider two men. Both have the same nature. Both (we assume) want to live and prosper. Both face the fundamental alternatives of life and death. These facts establish a kind of metaphysical equality between any two men.

Now, suppose that A tries to live at the involuntary expense of B, and suppose it is claimed that such an attempt is justified. Such a claim must rest on the assumption that A and B are unequal in some fundamental way, some way that justifies A's throttling the life of B. Unless it can be shown that A is somehow superior to B, his attempt to live at B's involuntary expense simply cannot be justified.

But there is no basis on which to claim, let alone prove, such inequality; the metaphysical equality that exists among men precludes it. Hence the attempt of one man to live at the involuntary expense of another is irrational—and therefore immoral.[71]

Lepanto's argument rests on the unexplained and unproven assumption that a man's actions "must" be "rationally justified." Lepanto has us suppose that A tries to live at the involuntary expense of B and that it is claimed that such an attempt is justified. But suppose, instead, that A tries to live at the invol-

71   Lepanto, *op. cit.*, p. 104.

untary expense of B and that it is *not* claimed that such an attempt is justified. What would Lepanto say about that? How would he prove that it is necessary to "rationally justify" one's actions?

In any case, it is not clear to me what Lepanto means in calling for "rational justification" of one's actions. For an egoist, the only "justification" for one's actions is that those actions benefit oneself. If, by means of reason, A concludes that he will benefit from living at the involuntary expense of B, then an egoist would agree that A is "rationally justified" in doing so. Lepanto, an exponent of Objectivism, is supposedly an egoist. But, for some reason, he expects some sort of non-egoistic "rational justification" for one's actions.

According to Lepanto, a claim that A is "justified" in trying to live at the involuntary expense of B must rest on the assumption that A and B are unequal in some fundamental (metaphysical) way and that A is superior to B. But for an egoist, as I've said, the only "justification" for an action is that it benefits him. Thus, if A is rationally convinced that he will benefit from trying to live at the involuntary expense of B, then he is "rationally justified" in doing so.

From this point of view, it is entirely irrelevant whether or not A is "metaphysically superior" to B. If I were rationally convinced that I could benefit myself at Lepanto's involuntary expense, then I would be "rationally justified" in doing so, even if Lepanto were "metaphysically superior" to me.

Of course, Lepanto does not claim to be "metaphysically superior" to me; he claims that we are "metaphysically equal." Why is this so? Supposedly because we have the same nature, we both want to live and prosper, and we both face the fundamental alternatives of life and death. But every living thing faces the fundamental alternatives of life and death. That doesn't mean that every living thing is "metaphysically equal," does it? And even though both Lepanto and I want to live and prosper, the chances are that one of us desires this more intensely than the other, in which case, are we "metaphysically equal"? As for the two of us having the same "nature," what this amounts to is that we are both human and, thus, share some biological traits. There is, therefore, some degree of similarity between the two of us, a higher degree of similarity than that which exists between either of us and any nonhuman thing. But similarity is not "equality." As Murray Rothbard has said,

> A and B are "equal" if they are identical to each other with respect to a given attribute. Thus, if Smith and Jones are both exactly six feet in height, then they may be said to be "equal" in height. If two sticks are identical in length, then their lengths are "equal," etc. There is one and only one way, then, in which any two people can really be "equal" in the fullest sense: they must be identical in all attributes.[72]

72   Rothbard, *op. cit.*, p. 4.

Of course, with the possible exceptions of identical twins and clones, no two people ever are identical in all their attributes. On the contrary, every individual is unique, not exactly like any other individual.

Biochemist Roger J. Williams has discussed in great detail the phenomenon of human diversity:

> Individuals differ from each other even in the minutest details of anatomy and body chemistry and physics: finger and toe prints; microscopic texture of hair; hair pattern on the body; ridges and "moons" on the finger and toe nails; thickness of skin, its color, its tendency to blister; distribution of nerve endings on the surface of the body; size and shape of ears, of ear canals, of semicircular canals; length of fingers; character of brain waves (tiny electrical impulses given off by the brain); exact number of muscles in the body; heart action; strength of blood vessels; blood groups; rate of clotting of blood—and so on almost *ad infinitum*.[73]

Furthermore, individual differences in behavior and personality are observable soon after birth:

> At the Menninger Foundation a few years ago two investigators, a psychologist and a psychiatrist, found abundant evidence of distinctiveness in 128 babies that they observed carefully from four

73   Williams, Roger J., *Free and Unequal: The Biological Basis of Individual Liberty*, Liberty Press, 1979, pp. 46–47.

weeks to thirty-two weeks of age. Everything about them was observed—from diaper wetting and soiling, to feeding, sleeping, playing, crying and bathing. Some babies were found to be bold; others were shy; some reacted quickly to outside stimuli; some were slow. Some were aggressive and persistent when reaching for toys, etc.; others gave up easily. Some babies were very regular in their eating, sleeping, or bowel-movement patterns; others were correspondingly irregular. Some could tolerate tensions and frustrations readily; others couldn't take it. Marked personality differences showed up as early as they could be observed.[74]

Thus, as Murray Rothbard writes, "men are not uniform…the species, mankind, is uniquely characterized by a high degree of variety, diversity, differentiation; in short, inequality."[75] But if, as a matter of fact, people are not "equal," then Lepanto's talk about the "metaphysical equality" of all men is merely metaphysical mumbo-jumbo.

If people, by their biological nature, are unequal, then egalitarianism is, as Rothbard has said, a revolt against nature.[76] But libertarianism, the advocacy of "a free society" in which people enjoy "equal freedom" and "equal rights," is actually just a specific form of

---

74   Williams, Roger J., *You Are Extraordinary*, Pyramid, 1971, pp. 69–70.
75   Rothbard, *op. cit.*, p. 5.
76   Rothbard, *op. cit.*, p. 11.

egalitarianism. As such, libertarianism itself is a revolt against nature. If people, by their very biological nature, are unequal in all the attributes necessary to achieving and preserving "freedom" and "rights," e.g., strength, courage, aggressiveness, persistence, determination, intelligence, etc., then there is no way that people can enjoy "equal freedom" or "equal rights." If "a free society" is conceived as a society of "equal freedom," then there ain't no such thing as "a free society."

AMONG THE EXPONENTS OF THE MYTH of natural rights, Ronald Cooney is decidedly one of the lesser lights.

Nevertheless, his essay "Natural Rights" is of interest because of its unique arguments. Its arguments for natural rights are essentially negative arguments, pointing out the supposed horrible implications of denying natural rights. Let's examine what Cooney calls "the ethical arguments in favor of natural rights":

> If it is true that men have only the rights the State has seen fit to give them, what is to stop the State, at any time and for any reason, from taking back those rights? Furthermore, how can we say that the State acts wrongly if it chooses to take that action? By the logic of the opponents of natural

rights, the Nazi regime had a perfect justification for recalling the rights, including the right to life of 6,000,000 human beings, and should not be condemned or thought evil for simply exercising the prerogative to which, as a state, it was clearly entitled. Thus, the denial of natural rights quickly resolves itself into a rejection of the ethical differences between governments, making a slave-state the moral equal of a republic.[77]

It is a fairly minor point, but Cooney is somewhat misleading in equating the denial of natural rights with the claim that "men have only the rights that the State has seen fit to give them." This is somewhat misleading because the denial of natural rights does not entail the denial that man may have rights in state-less societies. Such rights as men may have in state-less societies are a matter of custom, not "natural law," and may be called customary rights. And such customary rights can vary according to time and place, like state-granted rights and unlike supposed "natural rights." So, to rephrase Cooney's first question: If there are no natural rights over and above the rights the State has seen fit to grant men, what is to stop the State, at any time and for any reason, from taking back those rights? But one could just as well ask Cooney: Even if the people do have natural rights, what is to stop the State, at any time and for any reason, from taking back whatever rights it had previ-

77   Cooney, Ronald, "Natural Rights," *The Freeman*, October, 1972, pp. 630–631.

ously granted? Have Cooney's (and other Americans') supposed natural rights stopped the American State from taking back many previously granted rights? Of course not. The only thing that can prevent any state from taking back previously granted rights is the *power* to prevent it from doing so. And that is so regardless of whether or not there are any natural rights. So Cooney's question proves nothing about the reality of natural rights.

But Cooney asks another question: If there are no natural rights, then how can we say that the State acts wrongly if it takes back rights it has previously granted? Taking that question literally, I would ask Cooney in return: Assuming you are not mute, what's to stop you from saying that the State acts wrongly? Yet I don't think Cooney meant the question literally. I think he meant something like this: If there are no natural rights, then what "moral justification" could we have for saying the State acts wrongly in taking back rights it previously granted? This question I will answer bluntly: None whatever. But I will point out that if Cooney really thinks there is something to be gained by saying the State acts wrongly in taking back previously granted rights, then he *can* say that, even without any "moral justification" for saying it. Cooney apparently thinks he must have a "moral justification" for criticizing the State in "moral" terms. But if one sees through the myth of morality, one realizes that one does not need a "moral justification" (and that there *is* no "moral justification") for anything one does or says. Since nothing is "morally wrong," it is not "morally wrong" to say the State is "morally wrong" in taking back previously granted rights even though it really isn't "morally wrong" for the State to do so. Thus, the denial of natural rights does not preclude the expression of "moral" criticisms of the State.

But even if a denial of natural rights did preclude such "moral" phrasing, I would ask: So what? Making moral criticisms of the State is not going to affect the State's course of action. Cooney can condemn the State 'till he's blue in the face, but his protests will not dissuade the State from taking back previously granted rights if the State has decided to do so.

Cooney goes on to assert that "By the logic of the opponents of natural rights, the Nazi regime had a perfect justification for recalling the rights, including the right to life, of 6,000,000 human beings, and should not be condemned or thought evil for simply exercising the prerogative to which, as a state, it was clearly entitled." Cooney is obviously referring to the Holocaust, the supposed extermination of six million Jews by the Nazi State. It so happens that I am a skeptic regarding the Holocaust in general and the six million Jews supposedly killed by the Nazis in particular. But, for the sake of argument, I will assume the truth of the conventional wisdom about the Holocaust and will respond to Cooney on that basis.

So what about Cooney's claim that those who reject the idea of natural rights must conclude that the Nazi regime "had a perfect justification for recalling the rights, including the right to life" of six million

Jews? Well, I find it interesting that moralists like Cooney seem incapable of looking at things from the amoral point of view. They almost invariably present amoralism in "moral" terms. But it is only the moralists who think in "moral" terms, who think that actions are, or are not, "perfectly justified." As I've already said, if one sees through the myth of morality, one realizes that there is no "moral justification" for anything anyone does. So the rejection of the idea of natural rights does not entail the conclusion that the Nazis were "perfectly justified" in killing six million Jews. Rather, the rejection of the idea of natural rights entails the conclusion that the Nazi were neither "justified" nor "unjustified" in killing six million Jews.

Cooney also claims that those who reject the idea of natural rights must conclude that the Nazi regime "should not be condemned or thought of as evil for simply exercising the prerogative to which, as a state, it was clearly entitled." But here again Cooney is presenting the amoral point of view in "moral" terms. While the amoralist may not condemn the Nazi regime or think it "evil" for killing six million Jews, the amoralist would not assert that others "should not" do so. The amoralist is also an individualist and believes "to each his own." If somebody wants to condemn the Nazi regime or think it "evil," that's their business. Furthermore, it is particularly absurd to claim that those who reject the idea of natural rights must conclude that the Nazi regime was "clearly entitled" to revoke the natural right to life of six million

Jews. If there are no natural rights, then, obviously, the Nazi regime had no natural right to kill anybody. (Of course, as a matter of fact, the Nazi regime may have had a *legal* right to kill Jews, but that is irrelevant to the issue of natural rights.)

But suppose Cooney were right and every Jew in Nazi-occupied Europe had a natural right to life. I would then ask: What good did the Jews' natural right to life do them? How many Jewish lives were saved by their natural right to life? The answer, of course: Zero. According to Cooney, "Natural law …provides protection for individuals' rights from violation …by the State itself."[78] But natural law obviously didn't protect the Jews' natural rights from violation by the Nazi State. If all Jews of Nazi-occupied Europe had a natural right to life, yet the Nazi regime was able to kill six million of them, then, clearly natural rights are of no value whatever as protective devices. A bulletproof vest may protect a person against being shot, but a natural right has never stopped a single slug. A gas mask may protect a person against gas poisoning, but a natural right has never saved a single person from being gassed to death.

Cooney concludes, "Thus, the denial of natural rights quickly resolves itself into a rejection of the ethical differences between governments, making a slave-state the moral equal of a republic." To which I reply: So what? To deny that there are ethical differences between governments is not to deny that there are other kinds of differences between governments,

78   Cooney, *op. cit.*, pp. 628.

differences that can be of great practical importance. Cooney obviously wants to believe that a republic is "morally superior" to a "slave-state," and sees natural rights as providing a justification for that belief. But this is not really an argument for natural rights; it is merely a confession of what Cooney wants to believe.

And who cares what Cooney wants to believe?

Not I.

I'VE SAID THAT THE IDEA OF NATURAL RIGHTS is an unprovable assumption. In any case, those whose arguments I've criticized have not proven the reality of natural rights. All their arguments prove is the aptness of certain remarks made by Nietzsche in *Beyond Good and Evil*:

> What provokes one to look at all philosophers half suspiciously, half mockingly, is not that one discovers again and again and again how innocent they are ...but that they are not honest enough in their work, although they make a lot of virtuous noise when the problem about truthfulness is touched even remotely. They all pose as if they had reached their real opinions through the self-development of cold, pure, divinely unconcerned dialectic (as opposed to the mystics of

every rank, who are more honest and doltish—and talk of "inspiration"); while at bottom it is an assumption, a hunch, indeed a kind of "inspiration"—most often a desire of the heart that has been filtered and made abstract—that they defend with reasons that they have sought after the fact. They are all advocates who resent that name, and for the most part even wily spokesmen for their prejudices which they baptize "truths."[79]

When believers in the myth of natural rights argue for that belief, philosophy becomes *philosophistry*.

In the introduction to his book *Heresies*, Thomas Szasz writes,

> Most of the heresies in this book ...pertain to matters where language is used in two ways, literally and metaphorically; where the true believer speaks metaphorically but claims that he asserts literal truths; and where heresy may consist of no more than insisting that a metaphoric truth may be a literal falsehood.[80]

The true believer in the myth of natural rights speaks metaphorically but claims to assert a literal truth. The purpose of this essay has been to insist that their affirmation of the existence of natural rights is a literal falsehood.

If this be heresy, then make the most of it.

79   Nietzsche, Friedrich, *Beyond Good and Evil*, translated by Walter Kaufmann, Vintage, 1966, pp. 12–13.
80   Szasz, Thomas, *Heresies*, Anchor, 1976, p. 2.

The *New Libertarian* Debates

Author's Note

(2008)

THE MYTH OF NATURAL RIGHTS was originally published by Loompanics Unlimited in 1983. In 1985, Samuel Edward Konkin III devoted two issues of his magazine, *New Libertarian*, to a debate on "natural rights." The first of those issues (Vol. 4, No. 13, April 1985) included reviews of *The Myth* by Jeff Riggenbach (favorable) and George H. Smith (unfavorable), along with a piece by Murray N. Rothbard endearingly entitled "On the Duty of Natural Outlaws to Shut Up." Rothbard did not review my book, nor did he deign to mention it. Instead, he asserted that "anarcho-Stirnerites" and "anarcho-pragmatists"—unnamed except, perhaps, for Jorge Amador—should "shut up" for their own good.

The second of those two issues of *New Libertarian* (Vol. 4, No. 15, August–October 1985) included

"Natural Law, or Don't Put a Rubber on Your Willy," a spirited essay by the late Robert Anton Wilson, which commented on the aforementioned pieces by Smith and Rothbard. In a series of editorial footnotes, Konkin argued with Wilson's piece, criticizing his major points and indulging in occasional fits of what has since come to be known as "snarking." This apparently annoyed Wilson enough that he expanded his essay into a more detailed monograph of the same title, which would also be published by Loompanics Unlimited in 1987. Wilson's short book is an excellent and entertaining piece of polemical skepticism, and I take some measure of satisfaction in having helped to inspire it.

Also included in that issue were the essays "Natural Rights!" by Robert LeFevre, "Some Further Notes on Rights" by Jeff Riggenbach, and my own contribution, "A Reply to My Reviewers," in which I responded mainly to George Smith's criticisms of *The Myth*.

Natural Outlaws vs. Natural Lawmen

Samuel Edward Konkin III

FOR THE PAST 15 YEARS of recent Movement history, Libertarians have taken Natural Law as a given. With the exception of Benjamin Tucker and his few followers in North America, there have been few enough challenges to the foundation of our current ideology. Recently, Natural Law—and Natural Rights, a separate but related concept—have come under attack from several directions, all at once, seemingly concerted.

In the high condensation of Southern California, libertarian supper clubs have nearly all had speakers assaulting the subject: Charles "Chuck" Estes, an ex-Galambosian semi-LeFevrian, from a pure skeptical view; Harry Pollard, an anarcho-Georgist activist; and Spencer Heath MacCallum, who is pretty much the standard-bearer of his own mini-faction, descended from his grandfather, Spencer Heath. Robert

LeFevre rose to defend the concept at a supper club soon thereafter.

Meanwhile, in the East, Jorge Amador of SIL and the Libertarian Party (all the aforementioned are anti-Party) dredged up the rotting corpse of Pragmatism, John Dewey's curse upon American philosophy, and dressed it up as a new basis for *radical* libertarianism in a new, fairly well-done libertarian newsletter. Other partyarchs have rallied to his standard.

And then, Lou Rollins wrote a booklet, abetted by Loompanics, a publisher of mostly counter-economic manuals and inspiration. So the barbarians, so to speak, were at our very gates!

How important is this issue? It certainly does not prey upon the mind of most libertarian activists in the streets nor on the minds of those behind the quills either. And one can take all sorts of strategic counseling from this deviation, if it be such, judging by Amador's incredible, if innovative, claim that pragmatism *aids* recruiting to the hardcore. History, unfortunately, bears out the opposite case.

Libertarianism had a false dawn in the late nineteenth century, and what brought it down seems largely attributable to Tucker's abandonment of Natural Law for Max Stirner's subjective egoism. Tucker himself gave up on his anarcho-activism in 1907 and retired to France, where he saw the First World War at close hand and died just before the Second. Some—like me—see this as a loss of a quarter-century of his activism and an unnecessary Dark Age of libertarianism for sixty years.

20 paces? Turn. Gentlemen, draw!

Libertarians: Natural Outlaws Natural Bastards

Jeff Riggenbach

THE MYTH OF NATURAL RIGHTS by L.A. Rollins is an important book that every reader interested in libertarian theory should be sure to acquire. By comparison with most of the other works in whose company it properly belongs—Nock's *Our Enemy, The State*, Nozick's *Anarchy, State and Utopia*, Rothbard's *For A New Liberty*, Rose Wilder Lane's *The Discovery of Freedom*, a few others—it is sketchy and slight, hardly more than a pamphlet, really. Moreover, it makes no constructive case of its own, being content merely to punch holes in the constructive cases of others. Then too, it is too often too enamored of the easy cheap shot to bother with more difficult, detailed analysis. Nevertheless, it is important for two reasons: first, because what it attempts to do it does very well; second, because it raises a strategic question of inestimable importance to the libertarian movement. It lucidly and unflinchingly directs the light of critical intelligence on certain fundamental ideas that generally go utterly uncriticized and unquestioned in libertarian circles but must be examined critically if libertarians are to make a philosophically respectable case for their views, and it raises all these questions at the exact moment when it has the best chance of succeeding in redirecting the mainstream of modern libertarian thought.

The intellectual emperor whose nakedness Rollins exposes, the idea whose absurdity he unmasks, is, of course, the idea of natural rights. For the entire period of about two hundred years during which the libertarian idea as we know it today has received expression in Western thought, the majority of its exponents have based their otherwise various arguments for it on some sort of belief in natural rights. The majority but not all. From near the beginning, there have been dissenters within the movement. Max Stirner, the German schoolmaster and philosopher whose magnum opus, *The Ego and His Own,* was first published in 1845, has long been the most prominent of these. Others have included the turn-of-the-century individualist anarchist Benjamin R. Tucker, who fell, in mid-career, under Stirner's influence, and, in the contemporary period, the distinguished revisionist historian James J. Martin.

When such dissenters have expressed their reservations about natural rights, they have generally been met with some variant or other of this objection: "But if there are no natural rights, what is to prevent men from doing anything they like to their fellow human beings? What is to prevent oppression, slavery, and mass murder?" Accordingly, L.A. Rollins deals with this objection both at the beginning and at the end of his discussion. On page two of *The Myth of Natural Rights,* he quotes Objectivist philosopher Eric Mack's assertion that "Lockean rights alone provide the moral philosophical barrier against the State's encroachment upon Society" and replies,

> But a "moral philosophical barrier" is merely a metaphorical barrier, and it will no more prevent the State's encroachment upon "Society" than a moral philosophical shield will stop a physical arrow from piercing your body.

Then five pages from the end of his book, Rollins returns to this theme. He cites Ronald Cooney's argument that if men have no natural rights, then they "have only the rights the State has seen fit to give them." And if this is the case, Cooney demands, "what is to stop the State, at any time and for any reason, from taking back those rights?"

"But," Rollins retorts,

> even if the people do have natural rights, what is to stop the State, at any time and for any reason, from taking back whatever rights it had previously granted? Have Cooney's (and other Americans') supposed natural rights stopped the

American state from taking back many previously-granted rights? Of course not. The only thing that can prevent any state from taking back previously-granted rights is the power to prevent it from doing so. And that is so regardless of whether or not there are any natural rights.

As further examples of Rollins' approach, consider his discussions of two of the other most common arguments of what Samuel Edward Konkin III calls "the natural lawmen": the argument that natural rights obtain in the same sense and for the same reasons as such "natural laws" as the law of gravity and the law of conservation of energy; and the argument that human beings have rights because they need them in order to survive in a manner proper to human beings.

Rollins replies to the first of these arguments by quoting (with full awareness of the irony involved) that recently born-again natural lawman Robert LeFevre. "Here is a man who spends his life cheating, stealing and robbing others," LeFevre wrote not all that long ago in the *Rampart*,

> Is there something in nature which decrees that sooner or later he will suffer for these negative and unwanted actions? Studies indicate that there is no natural retaliation. While it may be true that some thieves will suffer; it is equally true that some will not. The miscreant has to protect himself from his outraged neighbors who

know of his excesses, but the rain and the sun treat him the same way they treat others. All the laws of nature behave toward the thief exactly as they behave toward his victim.

In reply to the argument that "rights are a necessary condition of 'man's' particular mode of survival"—the doctrine of the Randians—Rollins makes two points. First, he notes that it is not literally true that human beings "cannot function successfully under coercion."

"Consider:" he writes,

> All of us who live in state dominated societies and who are not members or beneficiaries of the state apparatus, are living under some degree of coercion, if only by virtue of being forced to pay taxes. Yet, despite living under State coercion, many people still manage to function successfully. Ayn Rand herself provided a good example of someone who was able to function successfully despite living under coercion by the state.

"Furthermore," Rollins writes, making his second point, "in so far as it *is* true that 'man' cannot function successfully under coercion, it is also true that *animals* cannot function successfully under coercion," so "a 'right' to freedom from coercion must also be a necessary condition of every animal's and every plant's particular mode of survival, inasmuch as every animal and every plant is vulnerable to being injured or killed by coercive action." Yet, "in that case, 'man' cannot 'morally' survive. To be 'moral,' he must not sustain his life since that means violating the 'right to life' of some other organism. Ironically, therefore, 'man's *right* to life' is inimical to 'man's' life."

Why all the quotation marks around "man," you ask? Because, as Rollins points out in a parting shot on the issue of man's survival *qua* man, "man" is

> only an abstraction and is not a real, living being. It is only *men* (that is, people) who live, not 'man.' And men are all unique individuals, with unique physiognomies, temperaments, metabolisms, body chemistries, personalities, mentalities, tastes, preferences, prejudices, talents, aptitudes, abilities, beliefs, desires, interests, values, and purposes.

Stirner, Rollins reminds us, saw "man" for what he was long ago: "not a person, but an ideal, a spook."

Where did libertarians ever latch onto such a nonsensical idea? Where did they get "natural rights" in the first place? From classical liberalism, that's where. Since the time of its first murmurings during the 1940s and 1950s—through the publications and other activities of men and women like Rose Wilder Lane, Ayn Rand, Murray Rothbard, Leonard Read, Frank Chodorov, and Robert LeFevre—the modern libertarian movement has seen itself as an outgrowth of classical liberalism, has formed allianc- es with contemporary classical liberals like Friedrich

Hayek, Ludwig von Mises, and Milton Friedman, and has claimed such historic liberals as the American Founding Fathers, Thomas Jefferson, and the Old Right critics of Franklin Roosevelt's domestic and foreign policies as part of the libertarian intellectual heritage.

This has proved unfortunate, for a number of reasons, for the classical liberals have never been libertarians, not if by "libertarian," we mean a consistent, thoroughgoing advocate of unmitigated political freedom for the individual. If this is what is meant by "libertarian," then a libertarian must inevitably be an anarchist, an opponent of the State as such; there can be no such thing as a "limited-government libertarian"—there can only be libertarians, who favor abolishing the State, and statists, who favor retaining it. Classical liberals favor a much smaller and weaker state than any other statists favor, but they do favor the State. They favor a coercive institution that is to be regarded as fully legitimate and respectable when it interferes with the freedom of individuals, an institution whose only function is to insure that at least some of the individuals within its reach will not be free. Classical liberals (and so-called limited government libertarians are really classical liberals) are statists, not libertarians. They are the most benign of all statists, yes, but they are statists just the same.

It has been noted by more than one writer that the State, whatever particular form it may take in a particular country or era, invariably wraps a myth around itself to justify its activities and make it the easier to win and hold the allegiance of its victims, which it calls "citizens." Thus, the State calls its acts of theft "taxation" rather than theft and asserts that the payment of taxes is voluntary, or even that it was the idea of the taxpayer originally, so that the State is merely acting as his servant when it robs him. Thus the State calls its acts of mass murder "war" instead of mass murder and asserts that its argument with another state is, in reality, an argument between the peoples those states oppress. Thus, as Max Stirner put it, "the State calls the violence of the individual crime; its own violence it calls law."

The liberal state does not differ in this regard from other states. It too propounds myths to justify itself and help assure its survival and prosperity. The most important of the myths of the liberal state for our present purposes is the myth, which lies at the heart of classical liberal thought, that the State is necessary to protect the "natural rights" of its subjects—that, in effect, it is necessary for the State to seize our money, prescribe or proscribe our behavior, and tell us what we can buy or sell in order to protect us from those who would seize our property, prescribe or proscribe our behavior, and tell us what we can buy or sell. Liberals have differed, of course, over exactly what things the State should be allowed to do. But they all agree that the State must hold a monopoly within its area on the provision of certain services, and they all, therefore, conclude inevitably that there are cases in which the State may imprison people, seize their property, and force them out of businesses in which they seek to compete with the State.

Is it really necessary to remind libertarians that John Locke wrote his *Treatises* in a frank attempt to justify not individual liberty but a new sort of organization for the State? Or that the Founding Fathers had no quarrel with slavery? Or that Mises approved of the military draft? Or that Hayek approves of taxation, transfer payments to the poor, and even eminent domain?

It is intellectually absurd to argue that because every individual is entitled to liberty, it is necessary that he be forced to yield that liberty to the State. Any theorist who begins with the idea that the individual must be free must conclude, if he follows his theory where its logic will lead him, that, as a matter of both theory and actual history, it is the State that is the greatest threat to individual liberty and that individual liberty can only be achieved through abolition of the State. The most thoughtful among liberal thinkers have always come to realize this sooner or later, of course; and they have ended either by rejecting the State and becoming libertarians or rejecting liberty and remaining liberals. Those among them who have themselves been statesmen—and I include in this group the American Founding Fathers—have taken the latter course and have thereby, it seems to me, cast fundamental doubt on the sincerity of their original devotion to individual liberty. One has only to read a book like Albert Jay Nock's *Our Enemy, The State* to begin wondering if men like Washington, Adams, and Jefferson weren't merely political opportunists who found the Lockean liberal ideas that were then in the air very convenient as a means of making their motives seem pure and making it easier to drum up public support for their self-serving *coup d' etat*. If they had been libertarians, they would never have created a new state to replace the one they threw out of the country. And they certainly would never have countenanced the Constitutional Convention of 1787, which made that newly created government even stronger.

Yet, most contemporary libertarians, even those who have abandoned liberalism for anarchism, continue to claim John Locke, Adam Smith, the Founding Fathers, and such 20th century writers as Mises and Hayek as central figures in their intellectual heritage. I suspect that one of their strongest motives for doing so is a desire to have the greater respectability and the larger public following of these liberal thinkers rub off on their own much smaller and less respectable movement. Indirectly, however, I believe such claims have only the opposite effect because they make a mockery of the libertarian claim of rigorous consistency. Liberalism is not a consistent position. Its principles must lead to rejection of government as such, yet liberals do not reject government. This means that at best they are inconsistent, and at worst they are mere court intellectuals, offering rationalizations for a particular variety of the State.

The point that classical liberalism is inconsistent is made in a workmanlike, if not particularly imaginative or lively manner by Ripon College political scientist Stephen Newman in his recent book on the libertarian movement, *Liberalism At Wit's End: The Libertarian Revolt Against The Modern State*.

As his title suggests, Newman assumes at the outset that libertarian thought is an outgrowth of classical liberal thought. He devotes more than half his text to discussion of Locke and Hayek and to criticism of modern day "limited-government" libertarians like Robert Nozick, John Hospers, Ayn Rand, and Tibor Machan. The only anarchists he discusses are William Godwin, Lysander Spooner, Murray Rothbard, and David Friedman, and his approach to their thought is to try to show that it too stems from classical liberalism. (In Rothbard's case, of course, he can convict the horse right out of the horse's mouth.)

Newman offers other arguments here and there in his book, of course. He argues that private economic power can be as much a threat to liberty as the State. (No, his grasp of economics is not what you'd call sure.) He argues that liberty can be meaningless or without value in the absence of equality. (No, his mastery of philosophical analysis isn't too impressive either.) And those who hunger—in these days when *Frontlines* and *Update* are defunct and Samuel Edward Konkin III has only increased the infrequency of his own publication schedule—for simple, unvarnished libertarian gossip will find much of interest in Professor Newman's book, for it is a portrait of our movement's major personalities and institutions as seen by an outsider. There are some curious gaps in the portrait (where is Robert LeFevre, for example?) and some odd bits of misinformation (such as the claim—soon to be true, rumor has it, but not true now—that *Reason* magazine is published in Los Angeles). But, on the whole, the professor proves himself to be well-enough informed. And his depiction of our little corner of the intellectual world makes entertaining reading for a few page-filled minutes.

But the main thrust of Professor Newman's book is its claim that libertarianism is merely a variant, an extreme version, of classical liberal thought and that classical liberalism is itself no more self-consistent or practical than any other political theory that seeks to justify government. In the latter claim, as we have seen, the professor is sadly right. And this means that if libertarians wish to make their doctrine intellectually impregnable, they will have to stop claiming the liberals of the 17th, 18th, and 19th centuries as their intellectual forebears. Does this mean that there is no libertarian intellectual tradition? By no means. It means that the true libertarian intellectual tradition lies outside liberalism, with writers like Stirner, Henry David Thoreau, Stephen Pearl Andrews, Benjamin R. Tucker, Emma Goldman, Albert Jay Nock, H.L. Mencken, Robert LeFevre (at least in most of his published writings), and Murray Bookchin. I describe these writers as "outside liberalism" because, though certain of them have intermittently identified themselves with liberalism (perhaps in order to cash in on some respectability-by-association?) and though certain of them hold certain myths in common with liberals (the myth of natural rights, for example), they all explicitly oppose the State. They have, most of them, learned a thing or two from liberal thinkers, for liberals have been prominent among the most creative and insightful analysts of how freely interacting individuals may lead an ordered existence without that order being imposed upon them from above. But the fact that libertarian intellectuals have learned from liberal intellectuals no more makes the libertarians liberals than the fact that libertarians have learned from socialist historians like Gabriel Kolko makes libertarians socialists. Libertarians are opponents of the State. Liberals, both classical and modern—and conservatives, whether neo or traditional, whether of the Old Right, the *National Review* Right, or the New Right—are apologists for the State. Fundamentally, libertarians have nothing in common with any of these others and no more in common with some of them than with others. Libertarians are unique and have their own unique intellectual tradition on which to draw. They have learned from statist intellectuals, but they cannot accurately be classified with them.

One major point remains to be made before this essay may be brought to a close, and that is a point about diversity within the libertarian movement. I have argued elsewhere that there is no one libertarianism but many because it is the natural and inevitable tendency of intellectuals, and particularly of libertarian intellectuals, to be independent-minded and to develop their own individual theories, drawing on the theories of earlier writers but selectively, honoring no pre-existing theory with unqualified acceptance. This being the case, it is inevitable that any intellectual movement will encompass a diversity of similar but not completely reconcilable views. The irreconcilable differences may be mainly on minor points rather than on major or fundamental ones, but they will emerge and they will remain. Even religious movements generate such differences, albeit more slowly because of the fundamentally authoritarian character of religious dogma, which advocates acceptance of the teachings of others without independent thought of one's own. In a movement such as ours, which stresses individual autonomy and self-reliance, such differences are of the essence. To expect otherwise is a folly.

How, then, can I suggest that libertarians abandon their desire to associate themselves with the classical liberal tradition? How can I argue that libertarians are not the intellectual progeny of the classical liberals? Some people who call themselves libertarians and are widely accepted as such (even by those of their fellows who believe them to be fundamentally wrong) quite obviously are followers of the classical liberal tradition. My argument is not that these "libertarians" should be drummed out of the movement but, rather, that they should recognize the intellectual problems they make for themselves—and for their anarchist comrades who share the name "libertarian" with them—by building their theories on the inconsistent bedrock of classical liberal thought. If they wish to create a really strong argument for individual liberty, there are other, better ways to go about it than by trying to repair the arguments of the classical liberals. The two books discussed above may help to make this more clear: the Rollins volume by launching a powerful, if preliminary, assault on one of classical liberalism's chief myths; the Newman volume by focussing on the fundamental inconsistency at the heart of classical liberal thought.

And there could be no better time than the present to clarify this issue. For the libertarian movement, as it enters the second half of the 1980s, is clearly in a period of transition. The disastrous rout of the Libertarian Party in the 1984 presidential campaign has left many libertarians, particularly those who had affiliated themselves with the Party, wondering what exactly went wrong and whether some new direction, some new redefinition of the movement's nature and goals, might be in order.

The answer to their questions, put briefly, is that the party was a mistake to begin with. It is, to say the very least, incongrous for libertarians to be running for public office and operating a political party. Had libertarians never fallen prey to the nonsensical notion that they are the intellectual heirs of the classical liberals, they would never have involved themselves in such a fruitless undertaking in the first place. And if they can be made to understand, at this critical juncture, that they have nothing whatever in common with the classical liberals, they might well abandon party politics in favor of some more appropriate tactic for advancing their cause.

On The Duty of Natural Outlaws To Shut Up

Murray N. Rothbard

SINCE ANARCHISTS AND OTHER LIBERTARIANS are, to say the least, an embattled minority, we have tended to be indulgent toward anyone and everyone in our ranks, even those who have been busily pecking away at the vitals of the libertarian position. Or, to change our metaphor, those who have been picking off stragglers as we try to continue our march against the State. Without going all the way with Orthodox Randians, who excommunicate anyone that makes a slight error over "concept" or "percept," or who confesses a sneaking preference for Bach over Chopin, I say it is high time to take off the gloves in the struggle against those whom Sam Konkin incisively calls "Natural Outlaws." (Or, as in the classic joke about Hitler in the bunker, "From now on, no more Mr. Nice Guy!")

For many years now, first as anarcho-Stirnerites and now also as anarcho-pragmatists, the Natural Outlaws have been firing away from inside their supposedly impregnable fortress of ethical nihilism, sneering at such fundamentals of libertarianism as individual rights and rational ethical principles. Since the Outlaws stand for nothing, they believe they can remain permanently blessed with the advantage of the strategic offensive. They are akin to some group who might, say, pester physicists with the demand "Nyah, nyah, prove to me that physics is a science!" If the physicist tries to defend himself, it is seemingly easy for the critic, secure in his ignorance, to keep up the verbal challenge. I remember once a young libertarian (who, characteristically, was soon to become a lifelong Orthodox Randian) saying to me, in all seriousness, "How do *they* [Establishment astronomers] know that the sun is 93 million miles away? To me it looks like a few thousands miles!" And how, indeed, could an "Establishment" astronomer reply verbally, unless to say, "For Chrissake, go study!"? And this is also the proper answer to those who challenge the existence of rights and moral principles. The standard rebuttal of the Outlaws that moral theorists or rights theorists differ among themselves doesn't wash either: so do physicists and astronomers, but this hardly means that no such disciplines exist.

The nihilists remind me of the classic bore at college bull sessions: "Nyah, nyah, prove to me that this chair exists!" Trying desperately for "proof" accomplishes nothing, of course, to wipe the mocking smile off the face of the Outlaw. In a deep sense, and on many levels, the proper riposte is to hit the Outlaw over the head with the chair. For one thing, the purpose of philosophic discourse is, or should be, to arrive mutually at the truth, not to engage in parlor games or verbal fencing. To engage in such games, to be a bravura pest for pest's sake, is to put oneself outside the realm of rational discourse. (But this, of course, is a moral as well as factual statement!)

It is high time, then, that ethicists and natural lawyers take the strategic and tactical offensive. The fastest and most thorough way of disposing of a philosophic enemy, as all good Aristotelians know, is to show that he is mired inextricably in self-contradiction. In this essay, I propose to show that anarcho-pragmatism and anarcho-Stirnerism (or at least *their preaching*) are self-contradictory and, therefore, wrong *on their own terms*.

First, the trouble with pragmatism, and especially anarcho-pragmatism, is *that it doesn't work*. And since pragmatists believe that the only truth is whatever "works," that settles that (setting aside such deep problems as the meaning of "work," work for "what," etc.) Take, for example, the severe criticisms that Jorge Amador, the guru of anarcho-pragmatism, bas made of the Bergland-Lewis Presidential campaign in his organ, *The Pragmatist*. Amador's critique is that the LP was (a) too gradualist and also (b) ideological. In other words, *his* proferred campaign would be radical anarchist to the hilt *and yet* non-ideological. That is, all talk of moral principles or rights would be tossed aside. Not only that: we could no longer call the State an organization of a criminal ruling class because "crime" itself is a moral and natural-law concept and presumes immoral criminals ripping off innocent victims. So what would an Amadorean LP campaigner talk about? He would confine himself to demonstrating the pragmatic virtues of the radical anarchist alternative.

But this is a tall order indeed. In fact, a virtually impossible one. The pragmatic radical anarchist is faced immediately with powerful critiques from pragmatic statists. He can show, for example, that anarchy would increase production, yield a higher standard of living, etc., in the long run. But in the short run, lots of the privileged, subsidized, or monopolistic would be cast adrift. All these short-run, and maybe intermediate-run, problems could only be offset by vague future benefits. But why, pragmatically, should everyone prefer the long run to the short run? What about the high-time-preference people, who thus challenge the Amadorean: "Look here, fella. I know the pragmatic benefits I'm getting from the current system. And I know, too, the headaches, the disruptions, the losses that I and lots of others will suffer during the lengthy 'transition' period. Even if you've convinced me that eventually I might benefit, these benefits are too chancy and too long-run for me to want to risk it."? And if the average person cannot be sold on radical immediatist anarchism, *a fortiori*, the criminal ruling class, those net beneficiaries of the State, they who might well be losers *even* in the long run, *certainly* won't be convinced. At *best,* the Amadorsymp will say, "Well, I admit this anarchism sounds pretty good. But pragmatically, to ease the transition and minimize the costs that even you admit, let's move toward the ideal very, very gradually." And we are back, willy-nilly, to the Republican or Democrat Party, the master "gradualists" of us all.

It is no accident, then, that Democrats and Republicans proudly *call themselves* "pragmatists." Sure, they believe in freedom, in peace, in free markets, in all the goodies, but these goals have to be approached, they tell us, piecemeal, by the groping push-and-pull of the democratic consensus. And we are back hip-deep in the *status quo.* "Radical pragmatism" of any sort, whether anarcho or Khomeino or whatever, is virtually a contradiction in terms.

But this is only the beginning of our story. For it is also no accident that never in history has pragmatism inspired any sort of radical or revolutionary movement for social change. For who in hell would join a radical minority movement, and commit him- or herself for life to social obloquy and a marginal existence, for the sake of 20% more bathtubs or 15% more candy bars? Who will man the barricades, either physically or spiritually, for more peanuts or Pepsi? Look at all radical or revolutionary movements of the 20th century, whether they be Communist or fascist or Khomeiniite. Did *they* struggle and move mountains for a few more goods and services, for what we used to call "bathtub economics?" Hell no, they moved mountains and made history out of a deep moral passion that would not be denied. What moves men and women and changes history is ideology, moral values, deep beliefs, and principles.

It is no coincidence, then, that even in the libertarian movement, the people who have stuck to it over the years have been almost exclusively the believers in rights and possessors of moral passion. The libertarian pragmatists, what the Marxists call "economists," have generally hived off to good jobs and have forgotten any movement concerns. And, by their lights, why not? Why not let the crazy ideologues worry about the movement and about liberty? The pragmatists, as usual, will just take what comes.

Anarcho-pragmatism, then, simply doesn't work. It cannot push radicalism among the public, and it cannot build a radical movement. All it can do is subvert, weaken, and, if unchecked, even destroy the libertarian movement that the anarcho-pragmatists claim they are striving to strengthen and promote. Objectively, anarcho-pragmatists can only function as wreckers of libertarianism. And since moral passion and ideology *work* and pragmatism doesn't, the anarcho-pragmatists have a pragmatic *obligation* either to convert to natural rights or, at the very least, to *pretend* to convert and then use natural rights and ideology as a weapon with which to build an anarchist movement. Objectively, then, and *on their own terms,* the anarcho-pragmatists have a solemn duty to surrender, to shut up about their doctrines and abandon the field.

The same is true of the anarcho-Stirnerites,

they who proclaim loudly that all moral principles and rights are mere "spooks in the head," internalized restraints upon their sovereign will. To the Stirnerites, only might makes right, and each individual has the right to grab whatever he wishes. It has always struck me as ludicrous for a dozen or so anarcho-Stirnerites to swagger around proclaiming that might is the only right. In any contest of might between the anarcho-Stirnerites and the State, who do they think is going to win? For a tiny minority to preach might makes right makes no sense whatever. In fact, what makes sense, from either a pragmatic or a Stirnerite point of view, is to proclaim one's absolute devotion to individual rights even if one doesn't believe it. And what in the world should stop a pragmatist or a Stirnerite from lying in this way? Surely not devotion to absolute truth, the denial of which is crucial to the nihilist creeds of pragmatism and Stirnerism!

The Stirnerite obligation, on Stirnerite grounds, to pretend to be a moralist and a believer in property rights runs even deeper than that. For who in the world will deal with or trust any person who loudly proclaims his contempt for property rights and moral principles? It should be obvious to the thickest Stirnerite that if he wants to pursue a ruthless, amoral policy of steal-and-grab, he could not do so by proclaiming Stirnerism to the high heavens. No, as Machiavelli counselled, the prince must pretend to morality and the Christian virtues while secretly practising the opposite whenever opportunities arise.

(Oddly enough, Machiavelli himself violated his own rule by proclaiming Machiavellism!) So, therefore, Stirnerism itself requires that Stirnerites shut up and pretend to be moralists and natural lawmen. And, once again, any balking at such pretense in the name of devotion to truth would, in itself, violate Stirnerism by surrendering Stirnerite self-interest to the constraining "spook" of objective truth.

But, you might ask, if the Stirnerites and pragmatists surrender to their own logic and shut up and pretend to be natural lawyers, would I not be worried that their seeming conversion to rights and moral principles might be mendacious and inauthentic? No. I would cheerfully embrace that uncertainty for an end to the pollution of anarcho-nihilism and its baneful influence upon the libertarian movement. Let them practise their pragmatic or Stirnerite rites in the closet if they wish; they will at least have been neutralized.

But suppose, after my demonstration of their bounden duty, the anarcho-pragmatists and Stirnerites pay no heed and keep sounding off anyway, as I strongly suspect will be the case. What will thus be demonstrated about the true motivations of our anarcho-nihilist comrades? Could it be, dare I say it, that they really don't give a hoot about the truth or principles of anarcho-pragmatism or anarcho-nihilism and that, like the guy at the college bull session, they are simply interested in calling attention to themselves and being a pain-in-the-rear for its own sake? And if so, and I fear we may be driven to that conclusion, then the treatment they will deserve will be metaphorically the same as the guy hit by the chair. For they will have shown themselves to be outside the realm of rational discourse.

They will be outlaws, indeed.

Roughing Up Rights

George H. Smith

THE MYTH OF NATURAL RIGHTS is a scathing, all-out attack on "natural law" and "natural rights" as *moral* concepts, especially as used by libertarian political theorists. Rollins considers the specific arguments of some natural rights advocates; I agree with some of his objections and disagree with others. But faulty arguments by particular advocates within an intellectual discipline do not allow us to dismiss the discipline *per se* as flawed or nonsensical. Otherwise, *all* cognitive pursuits would go down the drain, including the "hard" sciences.

Rollins defends a radical thesis: that natural law and natural rights, in a moral sense, are not—and cannot be—valid cognitive disciplines. That is to say, they cannot be knowledge-seeking enterprises because there is nothing there to know. This is the thesis that I shall briefly examine in this review.

Rollins claims that natural rights are a "myth." They are part of the broader myth of natural law, i.e., the claim that a moral law exists that prescribes human conduct. It soon becomes clear that Rollins rejects the idea of objective morality totally and that his rejection of rights is an application of this sweeping rejection.

What does the theory of natural law/natural rights do (or fail to do) to deserve this all-encompassing dismissal? Rollins says the following:

1. So-called "moral law" is not really "natural law" as a physical scientist uses the term. Moral laws say how people *ought to act*; authentic natural laws "describe how natural phenomena regularly *do* act." To call rights a kind of natural law, Rollins argues, is to use the term "law" metaphorically.

Comment: If "law," to qualify as a valid concept, must "describe how natural phenomena regularly *do* act," then this stricture applies as much to governmental laws as to moral laws. Rollins says that when his car was broken into and its contents stolen, no natural law restored his property. Fair enough. But there is a *positive* (i.e., State-decreed) "law" against theft, is there not? Did this "law" prevent the theft, restore his property, or apprehend the culprit? No. By Rollins' standard, therefore, State "laws" are as metaphorical and mythical as moral "laws."

2. The word "rights," as used in natural rights, is also a metaphorical misuse of the term. Natural-rights proponents talk about rights being a political trump card, a no-trespassing sign, a moral barrier, and so forth. But one cannot literally trump with a right, nor will a right stop trespassers, arrows, or the government. Natural rights, therefore, are "fake or metaphorical rights."

    Rollins calls on Thomas Szasz's contention that mental illness is a myth, that concepts of health and illness cannot be applied to the mind literally, only metaphorically. Similarly to Szasz's point that real illness pertains to the physical body, Rollins argues that "Real rights are those rights actually conferred and enforced by the laws of a State or the customs of a social group." Rollins continues: "In short, positive rights are actual, factual rights. Natural rights, by contrast, are rights that people supposedly 'ought' to have...natural rights are imaginary rights."

Comment: Here, the issue becomes even more confused. Real rights are those conferred by the State. But these "real" rights do not stop trespassers, arrows, or governments, either. They certainly didn't prevent Rollins from getting ripped off.

If Rollins wants to use a criterion to dismiss moral rights as metaphorical, then he should apply that standard consistently. His test to distinguish real from metaphorical rights demotes both natural and positive rights to metaphor and myth.

At one point, Rollins quotes Jeremy Bentham: "Right is the child of law; from real laws come real rights." But Bentham at least took pains to be consistent. Unlike Rollins, Bentham would allow no other meaning for "law" than a prescriptive decree by the State. Thus, Bentham categorically rejected the term "law" when applied to physical nature.

A natural law, for Rollins, describes regularity in nature. Bentham dismisses this usage of "law" as gibberish and would have placed Rollins in the same camp of irrationalists in which Rollins places defenders of moral law.

Rollins cannot have it both ways. If authentic "laws" describe physical necessity, if they cannot be violated, then positive laws are as mythical as moral laws. Governmental laws, unlike the "real" laws defended by Rollins, *can* be (and frequently are) violated.

If, on the other hand, "law" is used to describe State decrees (Bentham's procedure), then it cannot refer to the regularity in physical nature.

There is a sense in which positive laws may be said to constitute a "barrier" to (say) theft. If a potential thief *believes* that he will be caught and punished, this belief may deter him. But the same may be said for moral law. If a potential thief *believes* in the validity of moral law, this may deter him as well. Moral laws constitute as much of a "barrier" (more, in my opinion) to theft as positive laws. Both require subjective acceptance by the acting agent.

3.   Where does the idea of natural rights come from?

Why do people engage in such mythical non-sense? Rollins' explanation is nothing if not succinct: "In my view, natural law and natural rights are human *inventions* (not *discoveries*) intended to further the interests of the inventors." This explains why there are so many competing theories of natural rights. After all, "the many different inventors of natural laws and natural rights have had different interests to further..."

Comment: This is a peculiar claim indeed, coming, as it does, from a self-proclaimed demolisher of intellectual arrogance and pretension. Just where did Rollins acquire this information? How does he *know* the secret motives of *every* defender of natural rights? Is it not at least *possible* that *one* defender of natural rights—somewhere, sometime—defended natural rights because he believed the doctrine to be *true?*

If Rollins has the ability to peer into secret motives, then he might consider becoming a professional psychic. If, however, he acquires his knowledge like ordinary mortals, then it is appropriate to inquire where he learned this juicy tidbit.

Rollins stresses the conflicting claims made in the name of natural law. To this I say, So what? Conflicting claims occur in every intellectual discipline. These conflicts lead to argument and counter-argument, which is how knowledge progresses.

Suppose all defenders of natural law had reached the same conclusions. Would this lead Rollins to be more favorably disposed to its validity? Or would he then compare natural law to a religious dogma, pointing to its rigidity and artificial uniformity?

The diversity of natural law theories, strictly speaking, proves nothing. To the extent that diversity serves as an indicator, however, it suggests that natural law theory, far from being an irrational dogma (as Rollins suggests), is a vital, ongoing discipline.

Having discussed some mistakes and inconsistencies in *The Myth of Natural Rights*, I shall now make some general observations about natural law/natural rights theory.

Virtually every major defender of natural law (moral) theory has recognized the difference between physical law and moral law, between "is" and "ought." (We find it in Thomas Aquinas, for example.) Yet, critics of natural law still trumpet this distinction as if were a catastrophic discovery. Then they express amazement that their opponents do not roll over and play dead.

Generally speaking, the term "law," when used by defenders of moral law, has referred to a principle of *causation* in human action. If man is part of the natural universe, and if causal principles are discernible in nature (Rollins does not deny this), then why is it so incredible to suppose that we may derive causal principles relating to human action? Is human action somehow exempt from causation? Or is causation itself a "myth?"

Suppose causation does apply to human action. A formulation of these causal principles would then constitute "laws" of regularity. No "oughts" are involved at this stage. The causal principles of human action are a matter of knowledge; they are true or false.

The determination of causal laws is referred to by Aristotelian philosophers as the "theoretical" branch of ethical theory. Given that we have this knowledge, what do we do with it? Can it be applied to some desirable end or goal? This brings us to what the Aristotelians call the "normative" branch of ethics. This is where the "oughts" come into play.

This raises the complex question of whether individuals do, in fact, share any ultimate goals, or whether they "ought" to share such goals. The intricacies of this question cannot be explored here, but I will sketch a general approach.

Ethical theory should be viewed as one cognitive discipline among many. It is a knowledge-seeking enterprise, part of the cognitive division of labor. We generate theories when faced with unsolved problems. Theories, including ethical theories, seek out answers to questions.

When evaluating a discipline, therefore, we need to ask: What is the basic problem addressed by this discipline? What questions does it seek to answer?

This means that ethical theory may be assessed from (at least) three different levels:

1. Are the questions addressed by ethical theory—"What constitutes the good life?" "Do some principles of action lead to better consequences than others?" etc.—meaningful questions? Do they make sense?

2. If the questions pass muster, is any knowledge available that would help us to answer these questions? Can we generalize from our knowledge of human nature and causation and arrive at principles that can then be applied to human goals?

3. If the questions make sense, and if answers are possible, then why should any *particular* individual accept the answers as guides to action? This is a question of personal motivation.

I believe all these criteria can be satisfied rationally. I therefore subscribe to a theory of natural law that, when applied to social interaction, leads to a theory of natural rights.

I should be happy to defend this approach if the natural law debate continues in future issues of this magazine. But a defense is not necessary as part of this review. *The Myth of Natural Rights is* a lively piece of polemic, and it scores a few points here and there, but it is riddled with internal inconsistencies and fails to specify what, *in principle*, would satisfy the author as an adequate defense of natural law/natural rights.

Taking pot shots at a complex discipline is one thing. But more than this is required to prove that natural law and natural rights are a "myth."

A Letter

Sidney E. Parker

MURRAY N. ROTHBARD ASSERTS, in your April issue, that "Stirnerite" egoists are under an "obligation" to proclaim their "absolute devotion to individual rights" even if they do not believe in them. Rothbard may rest assured that if it suited me to make such a declaration, I would have no scruple about so doing. I am quite prepared to be a hypocrite when it is in my interest. But his assumption that I *must* be one and that, as an egoist, I ought always to profess to be what I am not demonstrates his inability to understand what conscious ("Stirnerite") egoism is about.

As an egoist, I pursue my interest with my satisfaction in mind, not in order to conform to a prescriptive ideal of egoist behavior formulated by Rothbard. If, with due regard to time and place, I tell the truth about someone or something, or if I find it convenient to associate with others in an "atmosphere of trust," then I am being an egoist and suiting myself. Rothbard may describe me as a deviator from the egoist ideal as he sees it, but the deviation exists in his head, not in mine.

Rothbard holds up as examples of a "deep moral passion that will not be denied" the communists, the fascists, and the Khomeiniites. I agree that these movements "moved mountains and made history," but since the mountains they moved were of corpses and the history they made was to change the "bad" into the "worse," I cannot see what he finds so admirable about them. As an unrepentant "Stirnerite," ready to follow "a ruthless, amoral policy of steal-and-grab" when it suits me to, I must confess to a preference for the regimes of the Czar, the Shah, and the Weimar Republic rather than for the regimes that succeeded them. (Incidentally, it is interesting to note that Mussolini, who in his youth was strongly influenced by Stirner, was the least ruthless of the fascist dictators.)

Rothbard's remarks are aimed at an Aunt Sally, but they are a fascinating revelation of the moralist mentality!

Yours sincerely,
S.E. [Sid] Parker
Editor, *Ego*

Natural Law, or Don't Wear a Rubber On Your Willy

Robert Anton Wilson
(Footnotes by SEK3)

PROFESSOR ROTHBARD'S ARTICLE "On the Duty of Natural Outlaws to Shut Up" is a very forceful polemic and has the same emotional power, and indeed the same structure, as a marvelous sentence I once found in a Ring Lardner short story:

"Shut up," he explained.

The persuasiveness of such "explanations" can be considerable, especially if they are delivered in a loud voice and accompanied by a threatening gesture with a baseball bat. However, in Rothbard's article, they are accompanied only by the literary expression of such noise and threat, i.e., by what semanticists call "snarl-words" (which are the rhetorical equivalent of waving a baseball bat), along with such original suggestions as the idea that the proper answer to certain annoying questions is to hit the questioners with a chair.

As I say, I do not deny the vigor of such argumentation, but I find it lacking in intellectual coherence. I do discern a kind of adumbration of an argument in the midst of Rothbard's territorial howls and roars, however, but I cannot be perfectly sure I have grasped it since the noise of Rothbard's anger tends to drown out the content of whatever he is trying to say. It seems to me, more or less, that the argument, such as it is, claims to show that stupidity is the best and quickest road to political success and that those who are not really stupid should at least *pretend* to be stupid since dishonesty is almost as good as stupidity if you practise at it hard enough. Now, I do not disagree with this at all; indeed, my own analysis of politics and political ideologies is exactly the same. The only difference is that I have just stated it as bluntly and offensively as possible, whereas Rothbard states it with a great deal of unction, or lubricating oil, to make it go down more smoothly.

What Rothbard actually says (in part) is "What moves men and women and changes history is ideology, moral values, deep beliefs, and principles," and "moral passions and ideology *work* and pragmatism doesn't" and that one who is not moralistic in this sense should "pretend to be a moralist" since that is good public relations. I do not think my sarcastic paraphrase above was unjustified, although it is admittedly cynical. Some of us, however, agree with

John Adams that ideology should more properly be called "idiocy"; we harbor the suspicion that the "deep beliefs" and "moral passions" associated with ideologies tend to make people behave like lunatics, or like badly-wired robots, and that strong doses of skepticism and "common sense" pragmatism have been the only factors that have ever produced any relative sanity or relative peace anywhere. We agree that the kind of dogmatic passion Rothbard preaches indeed makes for political success and has created history as we know it, *but that is precisely why we find politics and history so terrible and ghastly to contemplate.* Or, as one of James Joyce's characters says *in Ulysses,* "I fear those big words that make us so unhappy" because *that kind* of "history is a nightmare from which I am seeking to awake."

So, then, I agree, totally, with Rothbard's claim that what he calls "moral passions" and "deep beliefs" (which I call fanaticism and Koestler once called "deliberate stupidity") have dominated history, or such history as we have known, and that is precisely why I am leery, cynical, and very, very cautious about that kind of passion and that kind of belief. If I were aiming for success in ordinary politics, in the framework of the rules of ordinary history, I would follow Rothbard's advice, shut up about my more unpopular opinions, and pretend to the kind of passions and beliefs that, in my view, inevitably make people dogmatic and usually make them blindly cruel. But I am not interested in entering that neolithic and violent game at all; I am only interested in satirizing and undermining it so that others may see it as I do, come to their senses, and grow reasonably pragmatic, a bit more skeptical, and relatively sane and peaceful; hence, I will not shut up. Sorry, professor.

George H. Smith's "Roughing Up Rights" has another go at demolishing relativist or skeptical heresy, but, alas, he only presents a set of assertions without any arguments, although he assures us that he will later present arguments if anybody wants to argue with him. I can only comment that Rothbard and Smith in tandem make an egregious combination. Rothbard says we should shut up, and Smith says he is getting his intellectual ammunition together to wreak havoc upon us if we *don't* shut up, and to anybody impressed by resonant rhetoric, it probably looks as if they have driven my side from the field by uttering fierce war whoops and waving wooden swords. Sure, such nefarious noises would scare the lice off a Viking, as the Irish say.

However, as those archetypal experts on "moral passion" and "deep beliefs," the regents of the Holy Inquisition, learned eventually, we heretics are stubborn bastards. I refuse to retire from the field and will now utter some war whoops of my own. I hope the judicious will find them to contain more common sense and less noise than the fulminations of Rothbard and Smith.

To begin with, since I am not as clever as those blokes, I am not as certain as they are. I offer my opinions *as opinions*, not as dogmas, and I do not claim to refute absolutely the particular deity (or idol) that Rothbard and Smith are offering for our worship, Natural Law. I am an agnostic about that god, as about all gods, but I am not smart enough to be an atheist. I remain open to the possibility that this divinity, Natural Law, exists somewhere, in some sense, as the other gods may also exist somewhere, in some sense. Since I lack precognition, I cannot predict what might be proven tomorrow, or in ten years, or in a millennium. All I say is that, for a slow learner like me, the question is *at present* still open, even if Rothbard and Smith devoutly insist that it is closed, and that arguments like "Shut up" and "I'll prove it later" have only increased my doubts and suspicions.

Now, "Natural Law" in the sense of ideologists or idolators like Rothbard and Smith is quite distinct from "Natural Law" in the sense of the physical sciences.[81] A so-called "Natural Law" in the sciences is a statistical generalization from which predictions can be made that can be *refuted* by experiment. No experiment or experiments can *totally* "prove" such a statistical generalization, because we do not know, and cannot know, what surprises the future may hold,

---

81   George & Murray will defend themselves; however, many of us, especially myself, do use Natural Law in the "scientific" sense, or, as it was originally called, Natural Science. Wilson is uncharacteristically sweeping and dogmatic about what constitutes Natural Law in Science, though. Besides statistical generalizations, there are the fundamental axioms of Science that, like those of Praxeology, are *a priori* and irrefutable. Examples: Observations Exist, Observations may be integrated into theories, causality exists, causality can be observed, and so on. Without these *a priori* axioms, nothing else follows or could ever. —SEK3

but those generalizations that have survived a great deal of testing are considered relatively safe, or highly probable, and, therefore, have *"meaning" in* the scientific sense. Experiments may, however, *refute* a generalization, and that is why *the possibility of refutation* is necessary for any generalization to he considered scientifically meaningful. Propositions that have been so worded that they can never be experimentally refuted (such as theological doctrines like transubstantiation) are not regarded as scientifically meaningful.

"Natural Law" in this scientific sense, being only a set of potentially refutable predictions, has nothing in common with "law" in the ordinary sense, or Statute Law. Thus, the use of the word "law" in science has been recognized as metaphoric by most modern scientists, and many, especially the physicists of the Copenhagen view, regard it as a dangerous and potentially misleading metaphor.

"Natural Law" in the theological sense is quite different in virtually every respect. To take a typical example, the "Natural Law" in theology that has aroused the most hilarity in this century is that Roman Catholic principle which the Monty Python group has succinctly and colloquially stated as "Don't put a rubber on your willy." In the more resonant terms the Vatican prefers, this is more usually stated as "Contraception is against Natural Law." One immediately sees that this kind of "Natural Law" has nothing in common with the statistical generalizations *metaphorically called "laws"* in science. This Vatican "law" is not subject to experiment: experiment, and refutation by experiment, are irrelevant to it. The pope knows as well as you and I know that many Protestant males, Jewish males, heretical and free-thinking males, and even some Catholic males do, in fact, often put rubbers on their willies. That doesn't matter. This kind of law does not refer to physical, palpable events.

Ohm's "law" (so-called) holds that $E=IR$, or voltage equals current times resistance. This is a statistical generalization, and I personally came to understand *that* very intensely when working for five years as an engineering aide in my youth. According to Ohm's "law," if voltage is 10 volts and resistance is 2 ohms, then current should be 5 amperes. It seldom is, *exactly*. It is usually something like 4.9 amperes or 5.1 amperes, but sometimes it wanders around as far as, say, 5.3 amperes. This is explained, of course, by "instrument error," "human error," and the fact that conditions in the field are never the ideal conditions of the ideal (Platonic) laboratory. Nonetheless, although other engineers will agree with this, nobody wants to give up Ohm's "law," which is still a safe statistical generalization. If "law" in the scientific sense was like "Natural Law" in the theological sense, one would find the meters reading, in this case, anything from one ampere to a million amperes, and I would be as dubious about science as I am about theology. But as long as the meters only wander a little, we vulgar pragmatists accept Ohm's "law," if not as an Eternal Metaphysical Epiphany, then as a useful generalization that is statistically accurate *enough*, at least for unmetaphysical lowlifes like us.

To turn this comparison around, for even greater clarity, if theological "Natural Law" was remotely like such scientific generalizations as Ohm's "law," then we would not find millions and millions of males successfully stretching rubbers over their willies. We would find that once in a while, somebody *almost* manages to get the damn condom over his dingus but that, in most cases, it statistically just will not fit, and the Church's "law" would be refuted, in the scientific sense, whenever somebody actually got the rubber all the way over his willy.[82]

82 Allow me another interruption, with all respect to Mr. Wilson, whom I esteem very highly indeed. I'll keep them down here where I can most easily be ignored by those who want his uninterrupted flow.

What the Roman Catholics are saying, judging from my study of their version of Natural Law philosophy, is that there are Unwanted Consequences inevitably resulting (statistically, if you wish) from a given action. That I would agree with. The undesired consequence they perceive is, of course, a decline in the number of newborn Roman Catholics. Enforcement of anti-contraception (not, of course, of Natural Law, which is self-enforcing) does, to the extent they are capable of doing it, indeed lead to an increase in RC population. However, many of us would point out that this Enforcement also violates Natural Law, judging from the Unwanted Consequence (one assumes) of the Church losing as many educated, sophisticated Westerners to apostasy over this Enforcement as they gain in uneducated, unsophisticated children of like parents. Since the former category make much better Defenders Of The Faith, and since the latter—sorry, racists—keep turning into the former over time and a progressive economy, the RC Church from a Natural Law argument should either modify methods or abandon their position. One more point: Natural Law is historically the poor and oppressed person's defense against established churches and States. —SEK3

I know this is "Simple Simon" stuff, on a kindergarten level, but while Mr. Smith has not presented his argument for "Natural Law" in the "moral" sense, he has offered us a sketch of what his argument might be like if he ever gets around to presenting it, it seems to me that what he sketches attempts to confuse "law" in the *metaphoric* sense of scientific generalization with "Natural Law" in the theological sense; I am trying to de-confuse and differentiate them.

The basic difference between science and theology has not been stated yet. "Don't put a rubber on your willy" does not attempt at all *to predict what will happen* if you try to put a rubber on your willy as Ohm's "law" does try to predict what will statistically, probably happen if you try to get a million amperes out of a 5 volt/2 ohm circuit. "Don't put a rubber on your willy" merely means that you *shouldn't* put a rubber on your willy. You shouldn't, within the context of Catholic "Natural Law," because it will make "God" very pissed-off at you.

"Natural Law," in short, is like Statute Law, in assuming a Law*maker* (which science does not need to assume) and by assuming further that this Lawmaker is also an Enforcer. He has His own jail, which is considerably worse than any human jail, and it is called Hell.

From a skeptical, agnostic (not dogmatically atheist) point of view, this theological "Natural Law" seems like an abstracted form of Statute Law *based on sheer bluff*. That is, even though one cannot totally *disprove the existence* of the Catholic God (since He has been defined in such a way that no experiment can refute Him), the Church cannot *prove the existence* of said God either, and we are, in effect, being asked to buy a pig in a poke. Not surprisingly, the willingness to buy such possibly nonexistent merchandise is called "faith" and is praised as one of the greatest of all virtues by those who profit from it.

I repeat: For all I know, that God may exist somewhere, in some sense, although the rhetoric employed by His worshippers arouses dark suspicions. I return the old Scots jury verdict: not proven. (I believe that verdict was traditionally rendered when the jury harbored dark suspicions but were not yet certain.) I decline Pascal's Wager (a more elegant form of Rothbard's "pretend a belief if you don't have it") because I am not clever enough to understand such abstrusities, and, when I am uncertain, it seems to me the simple, honest thing is to *say* frankly that I am uncertain.

Turn we now to the gentiles. The modern form of the "Natural Law" doctrine is like the theological form in attempting to tell us what we should and should not do but differs from traditional theology by not invoking "God" *very* explicitly and by becoming civilized enough to not threaten us with barbecuing or frying or toasting if we have doubts about the matter. This is a considerable advance, at least in style and good taste, and I do not mean to undervalue it. Nonetheless, it leaves me severely puzzled because if "Natural Law" in the prescriptive sense does not derive from some explicit "gaseous vertebrate of astronomical heft" called "God" or "Jehovah" or "Allah" or something like that, I cannot imagine where the deuce it does derive from. At this point, I can only stand around with my bare face hanging out and make my ignorance public, like Socrates, by asking annoying questions, even if this makes Prof. Rothbard want to hit me with a chair.

"Don't put a rubber on your willy because God will barbecue you for it later" makes perfect sense to me, even if I don't believe it, because it is a law in the traditional sense of Statute Law. That is, it has exactly the same form as "Don't smoke pot, because we'll throw your ass in jail for 20 years if we catch you" or zillions of other brilliant notions Statute Lawmakers have created. Both of these *tabus* or commandments *make sense to me*, even though they have never constrained my actions, because I realize that they are attempts to control me by threat, and, whether I like that or not (I don't like it), *I understand* what is being said.

But if the Natural Lawist does not explicitly invoke the Cosmic Lawgiver called "God" and the Cosmic Jail called Hell and is not a representative of a "government" threatening me with the more limited Hells that human beings create and call "jails," I fail to make any sense of the statement that something I want to do is "against the law." If such a "law" is not explicitly attributed to a specific "God" or "government," then it is not a law in the usual punitive sense at all. And we have already seen that it is not a "law" in the *metaphoric* (and archaic) sense in which scientific predictions are loosely called "laws." So what kind of "law" is it? And why should we regard it with the *religious* emotions of "deep belief" and "passion" that Prof. Rothbard urges on us?

George H. Smith, to give him credit, does attempt, in his sketch of a possible future argument, to suggest some kind of meaning for such an abstract and unenforceable "law." His sketch of an argument, alas, seems to rest on an Aristotelian notion of causality, in which predictions are either true or false. But it has been known for over sixty years now that scientific predictions are seldom neatly true-or-false but have to be expressed with varying degrees of probability.[83] *Ergo,* even if fields like sociology could someday be made as rigorous as, say, quantum mechanics, they would still yield only probabilities, not absolutes, and it appears to be Absolutes (with a capital A) that the Natural Lawists want. And, of course, predictions (with whatever degree of accuracy) about what will happen, or will probably happen, are still in an entirely different area of discourse than *tabus* or commandments about what *should* happen. Worse: If we are guided at all by such predictions—e.g., "if I smoke pot, they might throw me in jail"—we are dangerously close to "mere" pragmatism, will have the curse of Rothbard on us, and are sailing dangerously

83   "[H]ave to be expressed" ...is the form of a statement of Natural Law. In fact, Wilson does tread dangerously close to sloppy science here; measurements in the micro-level require such probabilistic formulation, but scientific laws remain as Absolute as ever—including the Laws of Quantum Mechanics! —SEK3

far from what most Natural Law-ists seem to mean.

However, it is worth following this point a bit further. According to Smith, from scientific predictions about what will (probably) happen, we can deduce *how to act so as* to achieve "desirable" goals (probably). I will not complain that he has not defined "desirable" since he is admittedly only offering a sketch. Let us assume that he can define it in some manner that, miraculously, will be equally satisfying to you, me, Rothbard. Konkin. and the galoot leaning against the lamppost down the street. Then what? We have arrived at a set of *tactical predictions* that have wandered an unknown (but not very small) distance from the rigors of the *scientific* predictions from which we started. It seems to me that *increasing doubt* should assail us at each step of that path if we are honest with ourselves, and I again fail to grasp why this murky and probabilistic conclusion should be clutched to our breasts with the religious "passion" and "deep belief" that Rothbard preaches to us. I may be too cynical, but it also seems to me that, each step of this path away from experimental rigor, increasing amounts of *guesswork, wishful thinking,* and downright *prejudice* are likely to creep in. The only grounds for "deep belief" at that point is a deep emotional *need* for belief.

Again, the main reason scientific predictions (miscalled "laws") are so often so marvelously useful is that there is no religious attitude of "moral passion" and "deep belief" connected with them in the minds of scientists. They are all regarded pragmatically, tentatively, and with cautious skepticism. Dare I suggest that this is why scientists so often accomplish *what they set out to do,* for good or ill, whereas ideologists and idolators just as often merely degenerate into perpetual quarreling, usually childish, with other ideologists who have equally "deep beliefs" but in other Idols? (I speak here only of ideologists without government power. What they do when they get government power is the principal reason I agree with Adams about the close link between ideology and idiocy.)[84]

Let us assume that I am a brighter guy than I think I am and that my agnosticism is just the result of pathological modesty. I know this is an absurd assumption, but let us follow it a moment as a *gedankenexperiment.* Let us say that by many decades or centuries of observation (since I hope to live long enough to get the Longevity Serum when it appears), I am able to derive what *seem to me* a set of rules about the consequences of human actions, not just in the statistical sense of probably *mass consequences (which* is mere sociology) but even, wonderfully,

---

84   Bob and I obviously have been in two Alternate Universes. His description of scientists does not match my observations at all. Furthermore, I know of no historical case where faithful ideologists have ever attained power; those pretending to such sincerity who do achieve power quickly exterminate their truly faithful comrades (Russia, 1930s Germany, 1790s France) or drive them out of the political realm (American Federalists vs anti-Federalists). In sum, we Natural Lawmen charge that Pragmatism and Methodological Uncertainty are the tools of oppression, not, as Wilson and lesser persons than he assert, tools of liberation. —SEK3

absolute Aristotelian certainties about individual consequences (that approaches "morality," at least in the Buddhist sense of *karma*). I admit that I would be rather proud of such a job of work if I accomplished it, but I still would feel uneasy about *calling* my correlations "Natural Law" or telling people to *believe* in them *deeply. I* would call them Wilson's Theory (that's as far as my vanity goes), and I would ask others to take enough interest in what I have done to try to prove or refute the correlations. I simply cannot comprehend why the Natural Lawists, if they really believe they have objective knowledge of this sort and are not just rationalizing their own prejudices, do not take that modern, scientific, and modest attitude. I don't know why they want to hit us with chairs when we question them.

At this point, I begin to feel a lot more sympathetic than I have felt in a long time toward that most nefarious of all skeptics, the infamous Max Stirner. Whatever else he proves or fails to prove in the long, turgid, sometimes brilliant, sometimes silly text of *The Ego and His Own,* Stirner has at least posed a very interesting challenge in asking how many disguised forms of the "God" idea appear in philosophers who do not use the term explicitly. It certainly appears to me that, e.g., "God told me to tell you not to put a rubber on your willy" makes sense, whether I believe it or not, and might even *be* a *"Natural* Law" if there is such a "God;" but "My study of humanity and the universe has proven that you shouldn't put a rubber on your willy" looks like a theory, a hypoth esis, perhaps only *an opinion*; and it is hard to resist some Stirnerite suspicion that calling it, or ideas like it, "Natural Law", may be only an attempt, conscious or unconscious, to elevate *a theory, a hypothesis, or an opinion* to some metaphysical level where nobody will dare criticize it or even think about it.

This suspicion, that what is called "Natural Law" may well be somebody's opinion with an inflated metaphysical name pinned on it, grows more insidious as one contemplates the fantastic amount of disagreement about virtually everything among the various advocates of "Natural Law." Prof. Rothbard tells us that this means nothing because there are disagreements among physicists too, but I fear that this is a very misleading analogy. The area of physics where there is, and has been for three generations, the greatest amount of disagreement is, of course, quantum mechanics; and the disagreement there is different—vastly different, in quantity and quality—from the total chaos among Natural Law ideologists. For one thing, all the disagreements in quantum mechanics are about non-physical, or metaphysical, matters. *There is no disagreement at all about how to "do" quantum mechanics,* i.e., what equations to use in making predictions in particular situations. The disagreements are all about what the equations *"mean"* in a general, philosophical sense, in the area that goes beyond—and cannot be tested or refuted by—experiment. Nor is there any doubt or debate about the practicality of quantum mechanics, that is why, as Gribbin sardonically notes in *In Search of*

Schrodinger's Cat, the majority of physicists use quantum math every day without ever having to worry about those philosophical interpretations of what the math "means." And, while nobody knows how to answer (scientifically) those questions about the "meaning" of the math, everybody agrees on how to ask the questions that *can* be answered scientifically.

In the area of Natural Law, and Morality generally, there is no shred of such agreement about fundamentals, about how to get the results you want, about what "equations" (language structures) are useful, or even about how to distinguish an answerable question from an unanswerable one. The Ayatollah Khomeini says that a woman may not divorce her husband for sodomizing a camel but may divorce him for sodomizing her brother. I don't know whether that is a Natural Law or not, although it looks like Khomeini's personal opinion to me, but nothing in Natural Law theory that I have read gives me the slightest clue as to how to ask a question that might yield a meaningful answer about whether Khomeini's judgment on the relative undesirability of sodomizing camels and brothers is or is not a Natural Law. Meanwhile, the Vatican, who gave us that gem about rubbers on our willies, insists that divorce is against nature in all cases, even including sodomized brothers. (They have not yet spoken out explicitly about sodomized camels, but I think "all cases" covers that.) The Mormon pipeline to "God," when it ran through Brigham Young, brought back the information that polygamy was O.K., but more latterly it has brought back the information that polygamy is not O.K. The Arabs haven't heard that news and still practise polygamy, while the Vatican's infallible authority insists that monogamy is the only sexual pattern in accord with nature; meanwhile, most Americans, especially in California, practice serial polygamy, or one marriage at a time, except for those who have given it up entirely and are just living together. Baba Free John, who says he not only knows "God" but is "God," agrees with the Pope in insisting on monogamy for his followers but doesn't care whether these couplings are heterosexual or homosexual. And so on. And so on. To compare this to the philosophical, highly technical disagreements in science is like comparing ten drunks crashing around in a dark room with the differences in nuance and tempo between ten conductors of a Beethoven symphony. Worse, it is like comparing the aleotoric contents of a junkyard with the occasional differences between professional librarians about where a given book should be filed in the Dewey Decimal System.[85]

---

85 And yet, C.S. Lewis, the Rational Christian, deduces Natural Law from precisely the amazing amount of agreement between various codes for human behavior deduced by completely different cultures around the world. One must admire Wilson's ingenuity or tactical sense in reversing the usual argument, which is that the Natural Outlaws end up in Chaos. Since Wilson does not acknowledge the possibility that Natural Law is simply conceptualization of the objective workings of human action, he cannot consider the possibility that these various religious leaders are violators of Natural Law by their subjective impositions. Which, unfortunately, puts them in Wilson's subjectivist camp, perhaps the only sober one dodging the drunks in their common darkened room? —SEK3

There is also the problem that even when some Natural Lawists, like Smith, admit the vast gap between scientific generalizations and their "Natural Laws" or *tabus*, they still habitually use language and metaphor that blurs that distinction and creates the semantic atmosphere of a discussion of "law" in the scientific sense. I do not want to be uncharitable and accuse such writers of dishonesty, but it certainly appears that such linguistic habits create confusion; and I suspect the Natural Lawists confuse themselves even more than they confuse their readers. The worst source of this semantic chaos, I think, is the term "Natural Law" itself since it is rather obvious that nothing can ever happen that truly violates nature, at least as the word "nature" is used in science and, I daresay, 99% of the time in ordinary speech. It would be clearer, and possibly more honest, if such an oxymoron were dropped entirely and replaced by "Moral Law." It makes sense of a sort to say that "It is against *Moral* Law to put a rubber on your willy," whether one agrees with that or not, but it requires endless sophistry and metaphysical unction to try to make sense out of the claim that it is against "*Natural* Law" to put a rubber on your willy. The only things that can be meaningfully said to be against "Natural Law" are impossible things, like drawing a round square or feeding your dog on moonbeams and plant fertilizer.[86]

86 Or creating a society where no one produces and all consume? TANSTAAFL isn't an expression of Natural Law? Morality follows from Natural Law; hence, Natural Law protects us from pseudomoral statists by telling us when they are lying. An action violates Natural Law when the consequences

Basically, I am skeptical and dubious (not dogmatically denying) about "Natural Law" because I do not possess the *religious* attitude toward nature (with a small n, please). An old joke tells of a preacher saying to a farmer, "God has been good to your field." "Maybe so," says the farmer, "but you shoulda seen it when He had it to Himself." Although I do not quite agree with the almost Manichean attitude of my friend Arthur Hlavaty, who seems to regard nature as a combination of slaughterhouse and madhouse, *against* which, by great effort, a few humans have created a few enclaves of reason and decency, I do rather strongly agree with, e.g., Nietzsche and the authors of the *Upanishads* that nature transcends all human categories, or, as the Taoists say, it can only be described in contradictions (good–evil, beautiful–ugly, wise–stupid, light–dark, wet–dry, happy–sad, etc., etc., etc., and more etc.). Thus, I neither worship nature pantheistically nor despise it Manicheanistically but, regarding myself as part of it, claim the same "right" (in quotes) as any other critter, from the cockroach to the whale, to alter and adjust nature, as far as I can, to make it more satisfactory to myself. I therefore agree with physicist Freeman Dyson, who says that we should not accept the prediction (called the second "law" of thermodynamics) that tells us the universe must eventually run down but should rather seek ways to reverse that "law" and, as it were, "rewind" the universe to work toward

invoked do not in fact follow. I think it only, fair to point out, at this point, that Wilson certainly hangs around mystics a lot more than, say, professional atheist Smith. —SEK3 greater order rather than greater chaos.

It is for the same reason that I support longevity research and the quest for ultimate immortality, even though death appears to be very much a part of nature (or nature-as-it-is-without-human-intervention).

And, in general, although I love animals and often go into raptures over the singing of birds and sunsets, etc., a very large part of what I love and enjoy consists of human inventions, such as pure mathematics and certain music and a few dozen great paintings and poems, and the "cold and unnatural technology" (as ecologists call it) that has abolished smallpox in the 1970s, and enabled me to walk again after I had polio, and had made everybody in the industrial West (even the folks on welfare) more comfortable and healthier than most people throughout most of history. I even enjoy a sunset better when I am listening simultaneously to Beethoven's Seventh or Carmina Burana on that marvelous product of applied quantum mechanics, the modern stereo. Thus, the notion that morality also is a human invention, which horrifies the Natural Lawists, does not horrify me; it just adds to my esteem for human beings and the wonderful creative powers of the human brain.[87]

---

87   I take no back seat to Bob in cheering sooty smokestacks and their polyvinyl byproducts. Nature-without-(Wo)Man is the goal of the ultimate genocide. But that's not why Lawists oppose the "human invention" of Natural Law, Natural Rights, and morality. One is not ruled by non-contradiction (another statement of Natural Law), one simply must deal with it in order to express one's Will. Make no mistake; if morality is

Indeed, the idea that something is devalued or degraded if it is shown to be a human invention sounds rather theological to me and again involves Stirner's suspicion that some so-called Rationalists, are still unconsciously thinking in theological categories. If Bach invented his music, rather than receiving it from some "divine" or "Platonic" or at least trans-human source, that does not lessen the music's value but increases my esteem for Bach. If Jesus invented the marvelous saying in John 8:7, rather than receiving it from some psychic pipeline to Papa Tetragrammaton, that does not decrease the importance of the saying (which ought to be burned onto the backside of every moralist, with a branding iron, since it is the one they most often forget) but increases the stature of Jesus. And, for that matter, if the pyramids were made by people, and not extraterrestrials, the pyramids still manifest extraordinary intelligence and show that people can be astoundingly clever creatures.

In short, I do not think things have to be inhuman to be wonderful.

Finally, if morality is, as its etymology suggests—mores: customs—a human invention, then, like all other inventions, it is open to criticism, revision, improvement, and continued progress, like other arts and sciences.[88] In that case, the attempt to remove it

---

human invention, some humans will be enslaved to others. And that heresy is what we so rightly fear. —SEK3

88   Natural Law, notice, is not claimed as invention. It is discovered, not invented. It is immutable to the subjective whims of the State's Rulers. A morality based on invention is thus valuable for statism; one that is untouchable by legislators

from human contexts and locate it in some Platonic realm is not only "spooky" in the Stirnerite sense but profoundly reactionary. Since Platonic realms cannot be scientifically investigated (no experiment can refute them), this places morality beyond the most powerful analytical tool we possess. Since Platonic realms are traditionally thought to be timeless and unchanging, this tends to mean that *we* should go back to the medieval practice of *memorizing* rather than continuing the modern practice of *analyzing*; such an idea seems psittacine to me. And since Platonic realms are *inaccessible*, *timeless*, and *absolute* simultaneously, this means that morality derived, or allegedly derived, from such realms will be *mechanical* (*the* rulebook *tells* you what to do) and, therefore heartless and mindless. Think of the old farmer throwing Lillian Gish and her baby out in the snow in *Way Down East* and you will have a vivid image of what that kind of morality has traditionally meant, why Joyce "feared those big words that make us so unhappy," and why most educated people these days visibly *cringe* at the very mention of the word "morality."

There is a widespread impression in many quarters that libertarians are mechanical (and mindless and heartless) in the manner of that farmer *in Way Down East*. I don't know how that impression got started, although I suspect that the rather robotic disciples of Ayn Rand had something to do with it,

is favorable to anarchists. Platonism is usually a Subjectivist problem; it is rejected by the Natural Lawmen (including self) that I know. —SEK3 but I am quite sure (as far as an agnostic can be sure of anything) that the impression will never be corrected if we refuse to look into our own hearts and minds, if we ignore pragmatism and common sense, and if we follow Prof. Rothbard's advice to shut up, follow the rulebook, and pretend to believe Revealed Dogma, whether we understand it or not. That program may make for a successful mass movement (it usually does), but I don't feel it is what libertarianism means to me. Let us leave such tactics to gentry like the Nazis, the Marxists, the P.L.O. and the Irish Republican Army, who are really good at that sort of thing.[89]

89 Bob remains our biggest single draw; more new subscribers ask about him than anyone else (since Heinlein's interview in 1973–74). And the above tour de force shows good cause. His reversal of the traditional positions of Objectivists and Subjectivists took my breath away. A tactical genius. Unfortunately, I remain unconvinced largely for the same reason that Rand failed to move me: a lack of historical dimension in the argument. History teaches us that precisely the opposite relation between agnosticism/subjectivism/relativism and oppression existed. Deists used Natural Law to smash State/Church power by ruling God out of Divine Intervention (including Revelations to pope & prophet), for He made rules that He could not break. Atheism arose when Man/Woman asked, "Since when does Law need a legislator?" And Anarchy began with the observation that the sole purpose of State legislatures was to violate Natural Law. Still, Wilson puts up the best (not just rhetorically trickiest) Outlaw argument I've seen yet because, from opposite ontology, he arrives at the same anti-political conclusions as Orthodox Agorism (almost said Orthodox Heresy). —SEK3

Natural Rights!

Robert LeFevre

I HAVE LONG HELD TO THE VIEW that the concept of natural rights is both viable and necessary for human beings who choose to live in communities with others of their own kind. Since the purview of science is to learn through observation, and since the concept of natural rights is conceptual rather than concrete, the scientific method has appeared to most scholars to be unavailable when the subject of natural rights is introduced. How can anyone observe a concept, a body of thought, an idea? Ideas cannot be weighed or measured and, in consequence, escape systematizing.

I owe a debt to Sir Arthur Eddington for his *Philosophy of Physical Science*, wherein he uses this explanation:

[Thus] there are two ways of dealing with the

unobservables which have been inadvertently admitted in classical physics. One way is to reformulate our knowledge in such a way as to root them out altogether. The other way is to sterilize them; they can be allowed to remain provided that the assertions which contain reference to them remain true whatever value we ascribe to them—whatever result we suppose the illusory observational procedure to have given.

I propose to show in this paper that the unobservability of an idea can be sterilized and that such sterilization occurs if and when it can be shown that a given idea, once accepted within the mind of an individual, leads to a reaction that, to all practical purposes, is the same reaction all other individuals will exhibit when considering the identical idea. The idea cannot be observed, but the reaction to it can be.

What I am suggesting is that the presumed unobservability of what people have in their minds cannot any longer be presumed to be illusory or unobservable for the following reasons;

1. While it may be true that we cannot visually weigh or measure an idea by any known scientific method at the present time, we can discuss the significance, range, scope, and peculiarities of that idea with the person who has it. By learning to listen, we are able to observe the reactions of the person who has the idea to the idea that he has. The idea becomes observable within the

reaction of the individual.

2. Additionally, we are able to count the numbers of persons who favor or disapprove of a given idea. Thus, if we were able to find an idea the reaction to which was universally one of disapproval, then even though we have not queried every member of the human race, we could scientifically predict that were we to do so, disapproval would be the reaction found.

3. Conspicuous though it may be that the opinions discernable in the reaction to a given idea are subjective, and, hence, are shaded by varying value judgments, we may contend that sterilization has occurred when we find that *regardless* of the value judgments and the subjectivity of the persons considering the idea, the universality of disapproval occurs. Thus, whether the individuals who happen to be tested agree or disagree as to the significance, range, scope, peculiarities, or other variables in conjunction with the idea, they all reach an identical conclusion when the idea is viewed as *affecting them personally.* This appears to be the case despite the differences they may exhibit in terms of environment, genetic influences, intellectual attainments, age, religion, nationality, or station in life.

It is the purpose of this paper to show that the concept of natural rights is just such a concept and that when it is examined by careful observation of the reaction of the person considering the idea, every human being will exhibit the same reaction. When each specimen of a specific species will respond in precisely the same manner under a specific stimulus (idea), we are on firm scientific footing to claim that the observation has been purged of the subjectivity of value judgment and that it arises from each person's own nature. Thus, the cornerstone of a moral imperative is a "natural" human reaction, derived from human reality.

Physicists owe a debt of gratitude to Sir Arthur Eddington, but I would suggest that philosophers who are not physicists may be under the burden of an equally large obligation. Before leaving this savant I would like to make use of one of his illustrations.

He describes the icthyologist who casts his net into the sea. This scientist hauls in his catch and then proceeds to act like a scientist by systematizing what he has pulled in. He reaches two *generalizations* that are the "so-called laws" of nature: (1) No sea creature is less than two inches in length; (2) All sea-creatures have gills.

To quote Sir Arthur,

> In applying this analogy, the catch stands for the body of knowledge which constitutes physical science, and the net for the sensory and intellectual equipment which we use in obtaining it. The casting of the net corresponds to observation.

It is obvious to the non-physicist that the catch

in the fisherman's net is not a complete index of what the sea contains. So when he challenges the physical scientist, most particularly on point number (1) [above], he may very well be met with derision. Physical science is concerned with physical realities that *can* be observed, their conduct quantified and qualified and predictable conclusions reached.

Indeed, this has been my experience when I have tried to suggest that the scientific method could be employed in the areas of ideas and concepts. My opponents have usually had far more familiarity with the physical sciences than I have had, and, most particularly, when it came to natural rights, they have offered me much the same argument as the ichthyologist might offer, to wit, "You are talking about something that doesn't exist. What I am talking about does exist because it can be seen and counted."

Or to quote Sir Arthur one final time, "If you are not simply guessing [about the existence of natural rights], you are claiming a knowledge... discovered in some other way than by the methods of physical science, and admittedly unverifiable by such methods. You are a metaphysician. Bah!"

Perhaps it is not too early to point out that no human being has ever physically observed an atom. They are too tiny to be seen. In an actual observational sense, they have never been detected. In this instance, the physicist has built up an entire science predicated upon something he has never observed.

Sir Arthur is making the point clear. The physicist does not have to observe the atom physically if he can conceptualize its characteristics well enough to quantify its effects and to, thus, be able to predict its behavior under specific conditions.

Turning to the phrase "natural rights," the difficulty of dealing with it is quickly seen. The word "right" implies an element of morality arising out of nature instead of from custom, or religious dogma. What it apparently does, in the minds of my critics, is to set forth the proposition that I am seeking to prove that Nature has issued a decree concerning human behavior. Were that really the case, they contend, Nature (in this case, deifically personified), would punish us if we disobeyed its decree.

Since it is manifestly absurd to suppose that lightning will strike the individual who violates the natural rights of another, or, equally, to suppose that he will lose his job, his fortune, or suffer some other calamity at the hands of an outraged Mother, I marvel that my adversaries continually interject this element into the argument. They accuse me of having failed to prove the existence of an anthropomorphic, interventionist deity who has the task of punishing the wayward. I have never made such a supposition, found such an entity myself, nor am I impressed by any such suggestion. It seems, indeed, that it is my adversaries who have been impressed and who wish to use me as a whipping boy to exorcise some subliminal terror which still haunts their dreams and arises from some residual tracings of religion.

Nature, so far as I know, is not personified and does not object to how much of it is understood, used, or misused. If natural law is understood and cooperation ensues, nature will favor the cooperator. If misunderstanding or misuse ensues, unpleasant consequences may follow. But in the latter case, the individual brings the difficulty on himself; there is no natural supernatural interventionist of which I am aware.

If the concept of natural rights contains an element of morality, what is that element? It is the conclusion, reached by individuals in virtually all nations, races, climes, and conditions in life, that there are certain types of behavior people *ought* to have and still other types people *ought not* to have.

Those working in the moral theater, where ideas about the behavior of human beings must be discussed, are concerned with what *ought to be* rather than what is. It is their contention that there *ought to be* an acceptance of the concept of natural rights. They believe that in the world we live in, with its various political factions, its necessary dependency on property of all kinds, and its overarching systems of legalities and legal niceties, the idea of natural rights should be playing, and is capable of playing, a vital role. Indeed, the viability and usefulness of the term will continue until such time as we are wise enough to eliminate the apparent necessity of government.

But isn't "ought to be" the problem? If one examines the history of humankind, he will surely discover that at no time have any two cultures accepted the same specific ideas about what *ought* to be or what *ought not* to be. Some groups have practiced cannibalism; some abhor the practice. Some groups inveigh against theft and do not steal. Others inveigh against it, but steal anyway, and some may even applaud certain types of theft. Some tolerate murder under some circumstances. Some do not unless the government makes war. Then medals are brought to the breasts of the most effective killers. And some truly object to murder and don't practice it at all.

There has clearly been no consensus whatever on the type or kind of behavior that everyone would recommend. Hence, it would appear at first blush that the group containing those who declare there is no such thing as a natural right are correct. Unless we can quantify our data, or perhaps sterilize it, we are going nowhere.

Is there a moral "absolute"? If there is, it, too, would be a concept. And to my mind, the Libertarian community has come very close to enunciating it. It is the central theme of the Libertarian philosophy that aggressive force which violates the boundaries of the person or property of another and does so against his will is universally wrong.

Clearly, this is an opinion, a subjective point of view, a value judgment. And it is far from being universally accepted, even among those who call themselves libertarian. One of the difficulties relates to the definition of "aggressive." Example: If it appears that another person is going to attack you, should you attack him first to prevent him from attacking you? If you fire the first shot, is your attack aggressive, or does the stance of your opponent, who *ap-*

peared ready to attack, identify the true aggressor?

This question is certainly vital in terms of what could and does occur in the physical world. However, it finds no footing in the epistemology of philosophic examination. If the concept of natural rights is comprehended, a philosophic answer to the question can be found, regardless of what a given individual might decide to do in such a set of circumstances.

When individuals are asked if they approve of the violation of the boundaries of persons or the properties owned by those persons, a general ambivalence originally surfaces. Their reaction to this idea will usually depend upon whose boundaries are involved. If the boundaries of an "enemy" or a murderer, thief, rapist, or other criminal are asked about, the reaction will almost always favor boundary violation. If the boundaries of an innocent person or a child are included, then the same individual who favored violation of boundaries may very likely withdraw his approval.

But there is one way of asking the question concerning boundary violations that brings about a universal reaction of disapproval. If the individual being interrogated is asked about the violation of *his own* boundaries, all ambivalence disappears at once. Regardless of possibly guilty criminal conduct, age, or condition in life, he will disapprove of violations of his own boundaries.

By this process, we discover a predictable phenomenon. The universality of disapproval as an observable reaction to this one idea when applied to the individual concerning his own boundaries instructs us that we are dealing with human *nature* rather than with human value judgments. Indeed, it is entirely likely that a demonstration could be made that would show that no universality of either approval or disapproval has yet been found in respect to any other concept or set of ideas. Value judgments interfere with all other findings.

Since it can be demonstrated that, normally, it is part of human nature that human beings will universally react *differently* in respect to *all* ideas, we can contend that human ability and propensity to value or to devalue is part of human nature, too. Thus, human individuality is natural and part of human nature. Our individuality is demonstrated by the manner in which we value.

But with this one idea or concept respecting the violation of the boundaries of person and property, we discover another natural condition. It is a part of human nature to disapprove of one's own victimization. Indeed, it could hardly be otherwise. Observable value variables and disapproval of one's own molestation clearly arise out of human nature and are not provided by contract, by government, or by any other entity, human or otherwise.

Since scholarship has generally accepted the idea that human opinion varies on the basis of individual value judgment and this conclusion is derived from observation of human behavior, it seems astonishing that any should cavil over the same method of observation and the discovery of the same degree of universality when matters of violation of an individual's boundaries are involved.

We have established that there is a universality of reaction arising in human nature and concerning the boundaries of each individual's person or property. Ideas of the nature of property and property ownership may vary. But there is no apparent variation when the individual considers the violation of his own boundaries. Regardless of the variations of value found in respect to race, creed, and etc., etc., we have a universal, *observable* response: "Violating the boundaries of others may be all right, but *don't tread on me!*"

This is the natural consensus concerning human behavior. When it comes to human behavior we know what persons *ought not* do. That consensus arises out of the nature of the human being, who is sensitive to both pain and pleasure. This element of morality, which we have observed and classified, can now be extended to the idea of natural rights.

The function of the phrase "natural rights" relates to the purpose of identifying the person who is in a position to "rightfully" control a given physical property. Since the term is an abstraction, it is helpful to have a contrasting word or phrase against which it *can* he compared. The contrasting word, which embodies the necessary opposite meaning, is "privilege."

We do not require any further research to establish that human beings, by reason of their individual human nature, are endowed at birth with the natural ability to control their own persons and to exercise that control without violating the boundaries of other human beings. Nor will it be necessary to establish that human beings almost always develop the ability to violate the boundaries of others. This, too, although accompanied by value judgments, leads to the same observable truth we have already made.

The term "natural rights" is an extension of this moral, universally demanded conclusion respecting the behavior of all human beings. What it establishes is that each individual not only has the ability to manage his own energies and properties, he has the *right* (the moral prerogative) to do so. And it follows, logically, that if *each* individual has the right to manage his own energies and properties, no individual has the *right* to manage the energies or properties of another without the consent of the individual whose natural control may not rightfully be wrested from him. To attempt to do so, or actually to do so, would be in violation of the universally demanded moral dictum.

It therefore follows that any and all attempts or practices wherein the natural control of a person's energies or properties is taken from him by the violation of his boundaries, and a second party presumes to act for the first party and thus against his will, we have a *wrongful* action.

What becomes clear is that human beings have the ability to control energies and properties far beyond their natural rights. Nowhere does this extended *ability,* an ability that goes beyond moral approval, have such impact as can be observed by the actions of those persons employed by government. Why libertarians should be encouraged to abandon a term that has its principal utility right at the core of the struggle between what belongs to me, *rightfully*, and that which the government presumes to take from me without my consent and approval is puzzling indeed.

I wish to be able to point out that those in government may very well have the *power* to take my money, my property, my freedom, or even my life; they have no *right* to do so. While those in government are, thus, physically stronger than I and can readily overpower me, this does not make their *ability* to overreach a rightful one. I have a *natural* right, arising out of my nature as a human being and with which I was endowed at birth. This right is my natural ability to manage my own energy, my own property, and my own affairs without any violent boundary intrusion. While the government can grab my properties, it cannot take away my rights. It can steal anything it can get its hands on physically, but it cannot handle my moral position. There I take the high ground; I was endowed with it by nature, and government, as unnatural and vicious an organization *as* could well be imagined, has no right *or ability* to take my rights. They are inalienable.

Whenever the government seizes anything of mine, such seizure is, therefore, a wrongful act and a most immoral act as well. Even the people working in governmental offices do not approve of the forceful violation of their own rights.

This does not mean that an individual cannot

have his boundaries crossed in a friendly manner. Boundaries are crossed constantly by agreement or by contract. When this happens, the use of both terms, "natural rights" and "privileges," come into full utility.

The person who has a natural right over himself or a property that he owns is always in the position of extending a privilege to another. Thus, I can tolerate or even appreciate the behavior of those I know and love who may presume to make use of my energies or my properties. I am happy to extend them the privilege of so doing. I may even contract with them, or with a stranger, so that they may (with my permission) use something that belongs to me. I extend them a privilege. They rent or lease something from me.

But, in each of these cases, it should be noted that the natural right is of a higher order than a privilege. A privilege is special permission granted, by the holder of natural rights, to someone who has no rights in that given case. The right to the energy or property of the owner remains with him.

It should also be seen that no person can *rightfully* grant a privilege where he is *not* the owner. Any such grant of privilege is a usurpation of the natural rights of the owner. Therefore, the government has no natural rights. Only humans have such rights.

Government personnel, largely the legal-minded, have tried to usurp the term of rights for many years. They have contended that the government bestows rights, that all rights are a matter of contract, and that you have a right to vote, a right to an education, a right to an income, a right to a job, and a right to a hundred other physical things that can only be supplied largesse by actions of grand theft in which the rights of individuals are constantly violated. The government also contends that any of these "rights" can be taken from you if it serves the purpose of those in power.

This provides still another reason for insisting on the use of the term natural rights. Since rights arise out of the nature of human beings, as we have shown, government cannot remove them. Human nature would first have to be eliminated. Government very well may have the power to remove any kind of legal right it may have granted. I am sure this will not be the last word on the subject. But it is enough for the limited purposes of this particular presentation.

Kranky Notions

Jeff Riggenbach
(Footnotes by SEK3)

MY ESSAY-REVIEW of L.A. Rollins's *The Myth of Natural Rights* and Stephen Newman's *Liberalism At Wit's End*, which appeared in these pages earlier this year, may have misled some readers. For, like all shorter works on philosophical topics, it greatly oversimplified its author's position. Indeed, it scarcely presented its author's position at all, except by indirection and implication. Instead, it concentrated on describing Rollins' position on rights and on sketching my own understanding of the historical origin of the idea of rights and its function in the development of Western civilization.

What, then, *is* my view of natural rights? It is, very broadly speaking, utilitarian. *Not* Benthamite or Millian, not based in the doctrine of any particular thinker of the past whose ideas have been called "utilitarian" by himself or others, but *broadly* utilitarian, that is, based on the assumption that the root of all value is utility. I hold with Ayn Rand that "the concept 'value'…presupposes an answer to the question: of value to *whom* and for *what*?" Entities and actions are not merely good: they are good *for* something. Their goodness can be judged—can be conceived at all—only in the context of some goal(s) or purpose(s).

I call this approach to thinking about values "utilitarianism" because it judges goodness by measuring utility or usefulness in the pursuit of some goal(s) or purpose(s). Another word for it in technical philosophy is "instrumentalism."

Most of the time, Ayn Rand writes as though she too is an instrumentalist. She says, for example, that morality "is a code of values to guide man's choices and actions" and that "a 'right' is a moral principle defining and sanctioning a man's freedom of action in a social context." And since she has already argued that "value" is an instrumental, or (in my sense) utilitarian, concept, it would seem to follow that morality is the study of which means are most useful in achieving certain ends and that "rights" are general rules about what sorts of actions are most useful in achieving which sorts of specifically social goals. And this does seem to be exactly what Rand is saying when she writes, in a famous passage from John Galt's speech *in Atlas Shrugged*, that

> *Rights* are conditions of existence required by man's nature for his proper survival. If man is to

> live on earth, it is *right* for him to use his mind, it
> is *right to* act on his own free judgment, it is *right*
> to work for his values and to keep the product of
> his work. If life on earth is his purpose, he has
> a *right* to live as a rational being: nature forbids
> him the irrational.

Explained in this way, the concept of "rights" appears rational and objective enough. In essence, Rand seems to be arguing that to say of a person that he or she has a "right" to his or her property is merely another way of saying that, given the goal of realizing his or her individual potential as a human being, it would be *good, valuable* for that person to be allowed by his or her neighbors to keep whatever he or she has legitimately acquired (which, to Rand, would mean by process of labor or voluntary exchange). To say that murder violates a person's right to life is merely to say that it is *good,* for the purpose of having a society in which each individual is able to achieve the greatest possible satisfaction and happiness, to let every individual live and to refrain from killing him or her.

If rights are understood in this way, I find them perfectly comprehensible and intellectually unobjectionable. In fact, it is difficult to understand why anyone would find such rights intellectually objectionable.[90] Surely it is obvious that a human being

90   The sentence preceding the asterisk is typical statement of Natural Law. Since Jeff's quoting Rand, is it not fair to ask about that seemingly smoking "stolen concept" blatantly in

cannot survive as his nature dictates he must if he is shot in the head by another? Surely it is obvious, though less so, that a human being cannot live as well as his nature would otherwise make possible if he is denied control over that which he has made himself or acquired from another in a voluntary exchange? If this is all that is meant by the claim that human beings have rights, it would be nearly impossible to find anyone who didn't believe in rights. Given this understanding of the concept, I believe in it myself.

But, of course, there are and have long been advocates of rights who deny the instrumentalist approach and who talk of rights not as values we would do well to respect if we would achieve certain social goals, a certain kind of society,[91] but as "natural laws" in something like the same sense which that term has when it is applied to phenomena like gravity. As Rollins points out, however, natural rights do not seem to inhere inescapably in nature in the way that gravity does.

My own guess is that the idea of natural moral law and the natural rights that are supposed to is-

his hand? —SEK3

91   The Natural Law position, based largely on the empirical (or, if you wish, "scientific") work of Franz Oppenheimer, popularized by Albert Jay Nock and Rothbard, is that Society (I will stoop to a bit of neo-Platonism for this term) only exists if the Natural Right derived from Natural Law is respected. Each and every violation is a corrosion of Society until its ability to self-repair is overcome and Hobbes' War-of-all-against-all ensues. (The neo-Platonism is justified because we are talking about an Essence, "pure society," or that which makes society society.") —SEK3

sue therefrom originated as a metaphor. Such regularities of nature as the rule that what goes up must come down were first noted at a time in history when human beings were utterly dominated by authorities, either secular or spiritual, by the laws of deities and the laws of primitive states. So, early scientists, in search of a new word to describe the regularities in nature they were observing, hit upon extending the sense of the concept "law." If it was divine laws that imposed regularity on personal conduct and political laws that imposed regularity on social life, then it must be "natural laws" that imposed regularity on the natural world. Later thinkers noticed that human beings always live fuller, more satisfied lives when free than when enslaved. They called this regularity a "natural law" too.

In so doing, they were making use of the time-honored principle of metaphorical transference, which is one of the main means by which English words have gained new meanings throughout history. For example, the word "grasp" came to be used in the sense of "understand"—as when we speak of "grasping" an idea—by just such a method. Literally, to "grasp" something is to take it in one's hand(s). Literally, a mind is incapable of grasping anything. But when one literally grasps something, one is enabled thereby to hold it before oneself, focus one's attention upon it, and make use of it as one wishes. Similarly, when one comprehends an idea and gives it a name, one is thereby enabled to hold it in conscious attention and make use of it. It is *as though* one were grasping the idea.

Take another example. Literally, to "rip" something "off" is to tear it violently away from something (or someone) else to which it is attached. To steal something from someone is to take it away from the person and/or place to whom (or which) it properly belongs. For someone whose car or stereo system has been stolen, it is as though something that was *his*—his the way an arm or a leg is his—had been ripped off of his person.

One more example: When an organism's body is ill, it ceases to function normally and appropriately, at least to some extent. When a person behaves in such a way that one is led to suspect that his mind is no longer functioning normally or appropriately, it is as though that person's mind were ill. Literally, a mind, being incorporeal, cannot fall ill. But figuratively, it makes perfect sense to speak of "mental illness." (For an elaboration of this last example, see Thomas S. Szasz's *The Myth of Mental Illness* and *Heresies*—particularly the "Introduction" to the latter volume.)

The original literal meaning of the word "law" was "rules that must be obeyed." The word derived from earlier words that meant, roughly, "that which is laid down or set down and is, therefore, fixed." And, of course, for something to be laid down or set down requires that there be a layer or setter—an authority. Originally, the concept "law" was applied to the rules laid down by human rulers. Later, by metaphorical transference, it came to be applied to the rules laid down by divine will for the orderly operation of nature. As Raymond Williams points out in his invaluable reference work *Keywords,* the development of the idea of natural law in Europe was associated with a "tendency to see Nature...as an absolute monarch." For, after all, the forces of Nature, like the forces of monarchs, exhibited great power. Then, too, Nature seemed kinglike in "the apparently arbitrary or capricious occasional exercise of these powers, with inevitable, often destructive effects on men."

During the 17th, 18th, and 19th centuries, Williams observes, which was the period when the idea of natural law first came to dominate European thought, both scientific and social, "nature was altered from an absolute to a constitutional monarch" and "was often in effect personified as a constitutional lawyer."

The only problem with metaphorical transference is when we forget that a particular meaning of a word is metaphorical and begin to take it literally. Few people believe that our minds literally grasp ideas or that thieves literally rip things off of our persons. But many believe that minds can literally become ill and that there are regularities in human social life that *must* be obeyed in the same sense that the law of gravity must be obeyed.[92] It is this concep-

---

92 There demonstrably are social laws which that be obeyed in the same sense that the law of gravity must be obeyed by willful human beings. That is, driving off a cliff with my car and demanding the result be that I reach the other side as in an animated cartoon is a violation of the Law of Gravity. Similarly, defrauding my trading partners in an agora and expecting the agoric relations to continue unaffected is a violation

tion of natural rights that is properly regarded as a myth. Myths are metaphors that have come to be taken literally.

What, then, does it mean to say that human beings have rights? Either it means that they are so constituted that they will need a certain freedom from coercion if they seek to prosper, or it means that certain rules inherent in nature stipulate that human beings must not be coerced and that these rules must be obeyed.[93] The first of these propositions seems to me not much different from the argument for libertarianism advanced by writers like David Friedman, who makes no explicit references to morality and rights but contends that if people seek to attain the goal of a peaceful, prosperous society in which every individual has maximum opportunity to realize his or her own personal objectives, they will find it useful to organize their society around respect for individual freedom. Talk of "rights" in such a context is merely a more succinct way of saying the same thing.

of socioeconomic Natural Law. If I am discovered, it will go particularly badly for me, but even if I am not, the general collapse of trust necessary for ease of exchange will grow to my increased annoyance and frustration. —SEK3

93   Jeff forgets the (*degenerate*, as we say in Quantum Mechanics) case in which both are true. To see it most clearly, substitute *survive* for *prosper*. Or *exist*. Since humans who do not exist have no choice, we must assume that if the violation of one or more economic "rules" leads inescapably to human extinction, they must be obeyed. (Surely, even anti-anthropomorphists will concede Capital Punishment is enforcement enough?) And such "rules"—Natural Law—abound in Austrian economics. —SEK3

On the other hand, the proposition that "rights" are rules somehow built into the structure of the world, rules that somehow *must* be obeyed, seems to me both obviously untrue and of little practical use in persuading non-libertarians of the value of individual freedom.[94]

94 Undoubtedly churlish of me to insert footnotes to the gentlemanly prose of esteemed Mr. Riggenbach, not to mention Mr. Wilson before, but consider it a small step upward in (metaphorical transference) table manners from the usual fannish practice of boldly inserting disagreement or commentary in parentheses throughout the text. Jeff is indeed trying to converge the Outlaw and Lawman position here and (along with Bob W.) helped me understand that there is some legitimate base for the Outlaws' confusion in historical evolution of terminology. But what about actual practice? In fact, his concluding paragraph is a 180° reversal of past experience. A provable case that Nature is On Our Side does and will increase our persuasiveness. The most spectacular case is that of Friedmanite (*shudder*) economists proving to ruling statists that their economic policies violate Natural Law. —SEK3

A Reply to My Reviewers

(1985)

IN HIS REVIEW OF *The Myth of Natural Rights*, George Smith says he agrees with *some* of my objections to *some* specific arguments for "natural rights," while he disagrees with others. "But," he comments, "faulty arguments by particular advocates within an intellectual discipline do not allow us to dismiss the discipline *per se* as flawed or nonsensical."

Smith has a point. But it's a point that's beside the point since I do not claim that faulty arguments for "natural rights" prove the inherently flawed or nonsensical nature of "the discipline." Indeed, before I criticized arguments by Rand, Rothbard, Machan, and a couple of lesser lights, I approvingly quoted the opinion of James J. Martin:

There is no way of proving these things and

there's no way of disproving them. If someone wishes to maintain that he has these intangible things called "rights," well, what is one to say about it? You can't disprove it—but again there's no way of proving them either.

Does Smith disagree? If so, *why*?

In any case, if proof is possible and necessary in this controversy, isn't it up to the believers in "natural rights" to prove the existence of that which they believe, just as it is up to believers in "God," "flying saucers," or "The Holocaust" to prove the existence of such elusive entities or alleged events? In short, doesn't the burden of proof rest upon those who assert the existence of...something?

I note that Samuel Konkin has promised that Smith will be arguing "The Case for Natural Law 'n' Rights" in the issue for which I am writing this reply. Does this mean that, at long last, someone is finally going to prove the existence of "natural rights?" We'll see.

Meanwhile, Smith makes a number of points based on the erroneous premise that I regard scientific "laws" (descriptions of how natural phenomena regularly do act) as the only "valid" concept of law. Somehow, he has read quite a lot into the parenthetical distinction I made between two different meanings of the expression "natural law"—the scientific one just mentioned and the "moral" one. My reason for making the distinction was to make it clear that I was discussing and criticizing only the "moral" meaning of "natural law," not the scientific one. Although, now that Smith has raised the issue, I am, in fact, inclined to regard both senses of "natural law" as metaphorical uses of the concept of law.

To be clear, however, nowhere in *The Myth of Natural Rights* did I assert or imply that scientific "law" is the only "valid" concept of law. I did write that "Real rights are those rights actually conferred and enforced by the laws of a State or the customs of a social group." By the same token, I would say that real laws are those rules, regulations, commands, decrees, ukases, etc., which are actually enforced by members or minions of a State.

Smith mentions my anecdote about the cassette recorder stolen from my car years ago, never to be seen again by me. I recounted this anecdote to rebut Samuel Konkin's claim that "the natural consequence of invasion is restoration" in the same sense that the natural consequence of jumping off a cliff is falling to one's death. "But," counters Smith, "there is a *positive*, (i.e., State-decreed) 'law' against theft, is there not? Did this 'law' prevent the theft, restore his property, or apprehend the culprit? No. By Rollins' standard, therefore, State 'laws' are as metaphorical and mythical as moral 'laws'" Smith's conclusion, once again, is based on the erroneous premise that I regard scientific "law" as the only "valid" concept of law. So this argument against my position is not sound. Indeed, if, as I actually assert, State law is the original and literal meaning of "law," then there's simply no way that State law can be just as metaphorical and mythical as "moral law." Of course, as Smith's criticism indicates,

State laws may be "mythical" insofar as they go un-enforced by the State in question. But to the extent that State laws are actually enforced, they are most definitely real.

I will concede that, by the same token, natural laws may be "real" to the extent that they are actually enforced by some Natural Lawman or other. If George Smith should strap on his six-guns and start acting like a one-man State, enforcing "natural laws" by force and violence, he might give these "natural laws" the same sort of reality possessed by State laws. In that case, realistic individuals within Smith's "jurisdiction" would have to take account of his enforcement activities in calculating their own actions, just as they have to take account of the activities of any State whose arms are long enough to reach them. But, of course, enforcing "natural laws" by the same sorts of coercive methods States use to enforce their laws is not the same thing as arguing for the existence of a universally valid, objectively existing system of "natural laws."

Smith writes,

> There is a sense in which positive laws may be said to constitute a "barrier" to (say) theft. If a potential thief *believes* that he will be caught and punished, this belief may deter him. But the same may be said for moral law. If a potential thief *believes* in the validity of moral law, this may deter him as well. Moral laws constitute as much of a "barrier" (more, in my opinion) to theft as positive laws.

But I did not assert that State laws are real because they constitute a "barrier" to (say) theft. Rather, I said, in response to a statement by Eric Mack, that if "natural rights" are a "moral-philosophical barrier against the State's encroachment upon Society," they are a metaphorical barrier and not a real one.

Although State laws may indeed have some deterrent effect on potential thieves, for example, the reality of State laws consists not in the deterrent effects of those laws but in their actual enforcement, that is, in the actual catching and punishing of those who act contrary to the stipulations of such laws.

Perhaps Smith is to some extent correct about the deterrent effect of sincere belief in "moral law" (although I know from my own experience that such a belief is compatible with habitual shoplifting over a period of years). But how can we ever know to what extent people actually are deterred from thievery, for example, by their belief in "moral law"? Even if it were possible to identify with confidence certain persons as both sincere believers in "moral law" and scrupulous compliers with the requirements of such "law," how can we tell which is the cause and which is the effect? In other words, how can we tell whether they scrupulously abide by "moral law" because they believe in it or whether they believe in "moral law" because they have no desire to do what it forbids? Is there any real basis for Smith's opinion that "moral laws" have a greater deterrent effect than State laws?

But even if Smith is right in thinking that belief

in "moral laws" has great deterrent effect, this implies only that moral beliefs such as natural rights might be more useful than I asserted in *The Myth*. It does not confirm the objective truth of such moral beliefs.

In reply to my statement that "natural law and natural rights are human *inventions* (not *discoveries*) intended to further the interests of the inventors," Smith writes,

> This is a peculiar claim indeed, coming, as it does, from a self-proclaimed demolisher of intellectual arrogance and pretension. Just where did Rollins acquire this information? How does he know the secret motivations of *every* defender of natural rights? Is it not at least *possible* that *one* defender of natural rights—somewhere, sometime—defended natural rights because he believed the doctrine to be *true*? If Rollins has the ability to peer into secret motives, then he might consider becoming a professional psychic. If, however, he acquires his knowledge like ordinary mortals, then it is appropriate to inquire where he learned this juicy tidbit.

Very funny, Smith.

But since you asked, I found this "juicy tidbit" in *The National Enquirer* (for inquiring minds), in a column by Jeanne Dixon. Thus, contrary to your snide insinuendoes, my claim in no way implies any claim to psychic powers on my part. So there.

But seriously, ladies and germs, Smith has a

point. How do I know that each and every exponent of "natural rights" consciously intends to further his own interests, to feather his own nest, by means of expounding this idea? Well, when it comes down to it, I suppose I don't know it (any more than Smith really knows that belief in "natural rights" has some significant deterrent effect against theft).

According to Smith,

> Rollins stresses the conflicting claims made in the name of natural law. To this I say, So what? Conflicting claims occur in every intellectual discipline…The diversity of natural law theories, strictly speaking, proves nothing. To the extent that diversity serves as an indicator, however, it suggests that natural law theory, far from being an irrational dogma (as Rollins suggests), is a vital, ongoing discipline.

Smith is right in saying that conflicting claims do not *prove* that "natural law theory" is an "irrational dogma." And to this I say, So what? I devoted about two pages of *The Myth of Natural Rights* to illustrating the extent of such conflicting claims by citing numerous examples. I did not claim, however, that this *proves* "natural law theory" to be an "irrational dogma." I did assert, in agreement with the statement I quoted from another writer, that these conflicting claims indicate that "When libertarians claim that coercion is contrary to natural law (or the nature of man), they must realize that, aside from the truth or falsity of this assertion, such an appeal to 'nature' places them in a confused and nebulous political tradition." The writer from whom I quoted this statement, incidentally, was George Smith (haven't I heard of him somewhere?), from a book review published back in 1974. Does Smith's current position that "natural law theory" is "a vital, ongoing discipline" mean that he now rejects his earlier view of it as "a confused and nebulous political tradition?" Or does he now believe both?

Rather than discuss Smith's sketchy remarks on "ethical theory," I will wait for his forthcoming (full-blown?) argument for "natural law" and "natural rights."

For the time being, at least, I'm going to ignore Murray Rothbard's attack on "anarcho-pragmatists" and "anarcho-Stirnerites" since I am neither. I will simply point out that Rothbard did not respond to the criticism of his "natural rights" argument that I made in *The Myth of Natural Rights*.

Jeff Riggenbach perhaps overpraises *The Myth of Natural Rights*. In any case, I appreciate his appreciation of my modest venture in philosophical muckraking, and I see no selfish reason to contradict his assertion that "everyone interested in libertarian theory should acquire" a copy.

While Riggenbach's remarks on *The Myth of Natural Rights* give me little, if anything, to complain about, there are some points in his essay that I find questionable. Because of a looming deadline and space limitations, I am going to confine myself to asking a series of questions inspired by some of his statements. Here goes.

First, who (or what) is "the individual?" What does "unmitigated political freedom for the individual" mean in practical terms? Can we really be sure that "the State" is "an institution whose only function is to ensure that at least some of the individuals within its reach will not be free?" Isn't it possible for "the State" to increase the freedom of some individuals by limiting the freedom of some others? Is it possible to abolish "the State as such," as opposed to destroying one state only to see it quickly replaced by a new State? Has any State in history ever been abolished for good? If, as Riggenbach asserts, "individual liberty can only be achieved through the abolition of the State," does this mean that one should therefore advocate such abolition? Or does it mean that "individual liberty" is impossible?

Instead of an Afterword

Instead of an Afterword

(2008)

IF, IN THE QUARTER-CENTURY since the publication of *The Myth of Natural Rights*, George H. Smith, Murray Rothbard, Tibor Machan, or anyone else has succeeded in providing a proof of the objective, literal reality of "natural rights," the news has yet to reach me. I can't rule out the possibility. Such a miraculous event may have occurred. There has undoubtedly been much philosophical material published over the past few decades that I have never seen or heard about. But, again, if somebody, somewhere, has managed to set forth some unassailable proof that natural rights exist, I simply didn't get the memo. And so, I have not changed my mind. I still reject belief in the objective and literal reality of "natural rights."

(Incidentally, George Smith's promised case for natural law and natural rights—the one that Sam Konkin said would appear in the same issue of *New*

Libertarian as my "Reply to My Reviewers"—did not appear in that issue, nor did it appear in any subsequent issue that I saw.)

One publication defending "natural rights" that I have seen since the original edition of *The Myth of Natural Rights* came out is a literary oddity entitled *On the Steppes of Central Asia.* For some reason, I received a free copy of this book several years ago. It appears to be a novel—a novel largely consisting of philosophical and political dialogues—set in an imaginary anarchist society in post-Communist Mongolia.

Mongolia? Yes, Mongolia.

In any case, the author seems to be one Richard D. Fuerle, though his name appears only at the end of the book, while the name of the novel's protagonist, "Matt Stone," appears on the cover and the title page. Go figure.

Recently, I forced myself to plow through the thing (with a little skimming and skipping), just in case it delivered a knockdown argument for natural rights. But as far as I can tell, it doesn't.

The author—let's just agree to call him Fuerle— *does* espouse a natural rights philosophy. Indeed, at one point, one of the Mongolian anarchist dialecticians confidently asserts that rights are "discovered, not created," thereby flatly contradicting what I have long argued. But Fuerle's *argument*, such as it is, seems to rest on some unproven assumptions.

In one respect, Fuerle's argument is reminiscent of Paul Lepanto's in *Return to Reason.* Lepanto, you'll recall, is the guy who claims that people are "metaphysically equal." Similarly, Fuerle says that people have "equal moral status." But as far as I can tell, he doesn't prove it.

This is not to say Fuerle doesn't fashion an argument for his assertion. He does, sort of, albeit in a backhanded way, by trying to put the burden of proof on anyone who does not accept this assertion and act accordingly. Thus, starting from the unproven assumption that someone has a right to a piece of property, Fuerle submits that no one can prove that his (or her) desire to possess that piece of property should supersede the right of the original owner and, thereby, justify taking it away from him (or her). This is supposedly because it is impossible to compare the importance of the values of two different individuals (an idea that, if I remember correctly, comes up in Austrian economics).

But even if this much is taken to be true (and I'm not conceding that it is), so what? Fuerle, like many moralists, assumes without proof that, for some unexplained reason, everybody has to be a moralist, that each and every one of us is somehow obligated to *justify* our actions with moral arguments. He has not answered the question that I posed to "Mr. Morality," Tibor Machan, in *The Myth of Natural Rights*, to wit, *Why does everyone have to play the moral game?*

In this connection, I will point out that Fuerle relies on the assumption that whenever someone does something, he (or she) is supposedly expressing, at least implicitly, a general approval of doing that kind of thing. For example, if you commit robbery, you are supposedly expressing a general approval of robbery, so that, implicitly at least, you are agreeing that robbery committed against you is kosher. Of course, if you had good reason to believe you could commit robbery and remain undetected, this would not constitute a *practical* argument against committing robbery.

In any event, Fuerle doesn't prove this assumption; he merely asserts it. Nor does he pause to ponder certain possible objections to his asserted assumption.

Take the case of an athlete who sets an Olympic record. If performing a certain kind of action implies general approval of people performing that kind of action, this would imply that he (or she) approves of other people doing the same kind of thing, i.e., setting an Olympic record in the same event. But what if it turns out that the record-holding athlete in question is proud, intensely competitive, even egomaniacal, and that, consequently, he (or she) hates to be outdone? In this case, he (or she) assuredly would not approve of another athlete doing the same kind of thing that he (or she) has done.

Anywise, with specific reference to "rights-violating" types of action, Fuerle makes things easy for himself by discussing "rights-violating" acts, such as robbery, only in the most general terms. But suppose someone commits robbery only of the rich, thereby expressing approval only of robbing the rich, and not of just any Tom, Dick, or Harry (or Jane). Suppose, further, that this robber of the rich never becomes rich himself, perhaps because he opts to share his loot with the poor. In such a hypothetical case, Fuerle's argument that a robber's action implies approval of robbery in general, and therefore of robbery of himself, falls apart. And if there is any reason why one *must* think of rights-violating types of actions only in the most general terms and not in more limited terms such as in the preceding example, Fuerle hasn't bothered to tell us about it, much less prove it.

Another of Fuerle's unproven assumptions is

that a modified Lockean theory of the origin of the right to own land (mixing one's labor with the land) is the true theory. He fails to mention, let alone refute, competing theories of land ownership, such as those espoused by Robert LeFevre (claiming a piece of land and putting up a boundary marker to notify the world of your claim), Joshua K. Ingalls (temporary ownership of only as much land as you can cultivate by your own labor) or Henry George ("public" ownership of land with private profit-making users of land paying "rent," i.e., the famous "single tax," to the government). Neither does he mention American Indian societies that reputedly had no individual land ownership (no individual right to *exclusive* use of land). Nor does he attempt to prove that such societies were violating natural law and pissing off nature.

I suppose that's enough about Richard D. Fuerle and his unproven assumptions. At least for now.

Another occurrence following the publication of *The Myth of Natural Rights* was the publication of an essay by Hans-Hermann Hoppe in the September 1988 issue of *Liberty* magazine, allegedly containing an argument, if not for natural rights precisely, then for some sort of Lockean-libertarian rights. The "argument" seems to be that the mere fact that people engage in argumentation somehow implies that individuals own themselves and their homesteaded property.

In a "symposium" published in a subsequent issue of *Liberty*, Murray Rothbard joyously hailed Hoppe's "argument," calling it "a dazzling breakthrough for political philosophy in general and for libertarianism in particular." However, other participants did a good job of demolishing Hoppe's "argument." Check out the contributions by David Friedman, Leland Yeager, Ethan O. Waters, David Ramsay Steele, and Douglas B. Rassmussen.

One review of *The Myth of Natural Rights* that was, to my knowledge, unique was published by Pat Hartman in *Salon: A Journal of Aesthetics* (No. 21, 1993). In that review, she castigated me for ignoring "the law of karma." Thus, as Hartman explained this "law," if something bad is done to someone in this life, such as having one's tape recorder stolen, it might be punishment for something he (or she) did in a previous life. For example, when Gandhi was assassinated, it might have been his due for having assassinated someone in a previous life. Likewise for the Reverend Dr. Martin Luther King, Jr. And, of course, for the fabled Six Million Jews murdered by the Nazis, who might have murdered Six Million Nazis in some previous incarnation.

So, it follows that even if a dirty, rotten, amoral scoundrel should get away with murder (or whatever) in this life, he (or she) just might get his (or her) comeuppance in his (or her) next life, or the one after that, or…whenever.

It's true. I did ignore "the law of karma." I don't believe in reincarnation or any other competing version of the afterlife. I don't *deny* the truth of such theories, but, being that I've never been dead (that I recall), I have no firsthand knowledge by which to verify any theory about life after death.

Furthermore, even if there is such a thing as reincarnation, that would not imply the reality of "the law of karma." For Hindus, I suppose, reincarnation and karma are a package deal. But I'm not a Hindu, and I can easily conceive of reincarnation without any moralistic goody-two-shoes "law of karma" attached.

Has anyone ever *proven* the reality of karma? Pat Hartman didn't even try. As far as I know (though I'm no expert on Hinduism), karma is an unproven—and probably unprovable—Hindu dogma. And, so, I continue to ignore karma, as I expect I will in my next life as well.

Acknowledgements

(2008)

My THANKS TO Chip Smith, Bradley R. Smith, Bradley F. Smith, Arthur L. Smith, George H. Smith, George Utley Smith, John Caspar Smith, Cordwainer Smith, Adam Smith, Captain John Smith, The Smith Brothers, Nevada Smith, Winston Smith, and other Smiths too numerous to remember.

I also want to thank my family (what's left of it), everyone at the local food bank, Jess E. Stewart, Jeff Riggenbach, James J. Martin, David Botsford, Michael Hoffman II, John Hoffman, Tim Cridland, TGGP, Ace Backwards, Dennis Eichhorn, Bob Black, Jim Hogshire, Heidi Hogshire, Adam Parfrey, David Nestle, Ivan Stang, Pat Hartman, Justin Weinberg, Don Glick, Bezalel Chaim, Heather Benson, Jan Cadero, Audrey Vasiliou, Mike Hoy, Jorge Amador, Steve Schumacher, Steve O'Keefe, Ted O'Keefe, Tom Marcellus, Clarica Scott Laubscher, Fritz Berg, Sybil Rhea Cochrane, Diane

Frank, Peggy Farrell, Linda Abrams, Naomi Geschwindt, Manny Klausner, Bob Poole, Tibor R. Machan, Rick Mitchell, Adele Mitchell, Camille Ibbotson, Wendy McElroy, Nina Hartley, Taylor Wane, John Stagliano, Ken Gregg, Crystal Wilder, Mike Johnson, Frank Perkins, Roger Price, Darrell Little, Alan Short, Wayne Scott Nelson, Emily Zukerberg, Sandy Nelson, Anthony Joseph Russell, Hugh Hefner, Linda Burns, Anne Marie Gaylor, Dan Barker, Nick Bougas, Mark Frauenfelder, Bob Jarvis, Michelle Burns, Sharon Nickles, Ludeen Gunther, Miranda Bryant, Wilmot Robertson, Willis Carto, Larry Montgomery, Mark Corske, Christopher Winstanley, Chris Bates, Janet Bates, Chuck Hammill, Tom Richardson, Mike Jones, Edith Efron, Morris and Linda Tannehill, John Hospers, Desiree Cosette, Matt Crowley, Charles Barr, Diane Baker, C. Ann Baker, Bill Kennon, Ralph Vail, Raul Ruiz, Lex Baxter, Phil Demeir, Phil Groves, Tim Virkkala, Richard Geis, Robert Bloch, Alexis Gilliland, Jim Maher, Ralph Raico, Bill Moulton, Tony Lesce, Skye D'Aureous, Natalie Hall, Filthy Pierre, Vic Richardson, Boyd Rice, Doug Kennell, Butler Shaffer, Gail Higgins, Dieter Wendl, David Ramsay Steele, Suzanne Bruckner, Chris Tame, Jenna Jameson, Marian Kester, Robert Faurisson, Germar Rudolf, Lawrence Wolf, Dave Schulz, John Boardman, Crom Carmichael, Shirley MacLaine, David Gordon, Mike Uptegrove, Walter Mikaloczak, Crystal Tipton, Sharon Outhouse, Melanie Iszley, and Rachel Iszley.

And of course, above all, I want to thank Allah for everything. I wouldn't want to be a perfidious ungrateful (wretch).

Recommended Reading

(1983)

Badcock, John, *Slaves to Duty* Laurence Labadie edition, n.d.
    It has been reprinted a number of times.
Browne, Harry, *How I Found Freedom in an Unfree World*,
    Avon, 1974.
Ellis, Albert, *Is Objectivism a Religion?*, Lyle Stuart, 1968.
Goodson, John A., and David M. Longinotti, "Those
    'Natural' Rights Aren't," *Reason*, September 1977.
Harland, John, *Word Controlled Humans*, Sovereign, 1981.
Hertz, Robert S., "Darwinist Libertarianism," *Loompanics
    Unlimited 1982 Main Catalog*.
Kaufmann, Walter, *Without Guilt and Justice: From Decido-
    phobia to Autonomy*, Dell, 1973.
Labadie, Laurence, *Selected Essays*, Ralph Myles, 1978.
Mackie, J.L., *Ethics: Inventing Right and Wrong*, Penguin,
    1977.
Martin, James J., "Introducing Revisionism: An Interview
    with James J. Martin," *Reason*, January 1976.
Mavrodes, George L., "A Challenge to Self-Ownership,"
    Reason, March 1970.
Nietzsche, Friedrich, *The Antichrist*, translated by
    H.L. Mencken, Noontide, 1980.

Nietzsche, Friedrich, *Beyond Good and Evil*, translated by Walter Kaufmann, Vintage, 1966.

Nietzsche, Friedrich, *On the Genealogy of Morals*, translated by Walter Kaufmann, Vintage, 1967.

Nietzsche, Friedrich, *The Will to Power*, edited by Walter Kaufmann, Vintage, 1968.

Olson, Robert G., *The Morality of Self-Interest*, Harcourt, Brace & World, 1965.

Rand, Ayn, "Casuality Versus Duty," *The Objectivist*, July 1970.

Resch, H. George, *Human Variation and Individuality*, Institute for Humane Studies, 1978.

Riggenbach, Jeff, "In Praise of Decadence," *The Libertarian Review*, February 1979.

Robbins, John W., *Answer to Ayn Rand*, self-published, 1974.

Rollins, L.A., "The Holocaust as Sacred Cow," *The Journal of Historical Review*, Spring 1983.

Roseman, Herbert C., "Natural Rights," *A Way Out*, October 1967.

Smith, George H., *Atheism: The Case Against God*, Nash, 1974.

Smith, George H., "Ayn Rand and the Right to Life: A Critical Evaluation," *Invictus* 17 and 18.

Smith, George H., "Objectivism as a Religion," *Invictus* 24, 25 and 26.

Stirner, Max, *The Ego and His Own*, Libertarian Book Club, 1963.

Swan, George S., "Discord in Utopia," *Reason*, October 1976.

Szasz, Thomas, *Heresies*, Anchor, 1976.

Walker, James L., *The Philosophy of Egoism*, Katherine Walker, 1905.

Williams, Roger J., *Free and Unequal: The Biological Basis of Individual Liberty*, Liberty Press, 1979.

Williams, Roger J., *You Are Extraordinary*, Pyramid, 1971.

Xerinye, Krista and N. Strakon, "Every Man for Himself," *Invictus* 15.

Cover Gallery

The Myth of Natural Rights by L.A. Rollins
Loompanics Unlimited (Port Townsend, WA), 1983

New Libertarian Vol. 4, No. 13, April 1985
Edited by Samuel Edward Konkin III

New Libertarian Vol. 4, No. 15, August-October 1985
Edited by Samuel Edward Konkin III

Natural Law by Robert Anton Wilson
Loompanics Unlimited (Port Townsend, WA), 1985

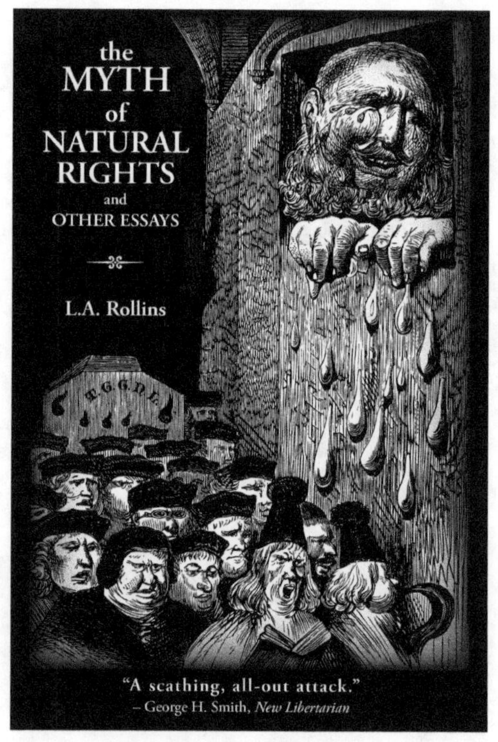

The Myth of Natural Rights
and Other Essays by L.A. Rollins
Nine-Banded Books (Charleston, WV), 2008